Common Knowledge About
CHINESE GEOGRAPHY

中国地理常识

（中英对照）

国务院侨务办公室
The Overseas Chinese Affairs Office of
the State Council

国家汉语国际推广领导小组办公室
The Office of Chinese Language
Council International

高等教育出版社
Higher Education Press

前 言

　　《中国文化常识》、《中国历史常识》和《中国地理常识》是由中华人民共和国国务院侨务办公室组织北京华文学院、南京师范大学和安徽师范大学编写的一套汉语教学辅助读物，供海外华裔青少年通过课堂学习或自学的方式了解中国文化、历史、地理常识，同时供家长辅导孩子学习使用，在海外反响很好。

　　近年来，随着中国经济社会的迅速发展和国际影响的不断扩大，海外学习汉语的人数，尤其是非华裔汉语学习者人数大幅度增加。为了进一步适应广大海外汉语学习者了解中国文化的需求，促进中外文化交流，中华人民共和国国务院侨务办公室授权中国国家汉语国际推广领导小组办公室对《中国文化常识》、《中国历史常识》和《中国地理常识》进行改编。

　　《中国文化常识》、《中国历史常识》和《中国地理常识》改编本是一套面向世界各国汉语学习者的普及型、口语化的文化辅助读物，适用于海外对中国文化和汉语感兴趣的各类人员。在中华人民共和国国务院侨务办公室编写的中英文对照版基础上，此次改编增加了中文与德、法、日、韩、俄、泰、西班牙、阿拉伯语的对照版本。

　　中国国家汉语国际推广领导小组办公室委托高等教育出版社对《中国文化常识》、《中国历史常识》和《中国地理常识》进行改编，高等教育出版社对原书的部分内容进行了增删，修订了部分数据，重新遴选和修改了插图，并翻译出版英、德、泰语版本；外语教学与研究出版社翻译出版法、日、韩语版本；华语教学出版社翻译出版俄、西班牙、阿拉伯语版本。此次改编力求在原书强调科学性、思想性和实用性的基础上做进一步创新。希望本系列读物成为您了解中国的窗口，成为您通向汉语世界的桥梁。

　　此次改编得到了海内外诸多专家、学者和教师的关心与支持，他们提出了许多中肯的建议，在此向他们表示诚挚的谢意。

　　由于时间所限，书中不免会有疏漏和不当之处，希望使用者和专家学者不吝赐正，以供今后修订时改正。

中国国家汉语国际推广领导小组办公室

2006 年 11 月

Preface

Common Knowledge About Chinese Culture, Common Knowledge About Chinese History and Common Knowledge About Chinese Geography are a series of readers initiated by the Overseas Chinese Affairs Office of the State Council of the People's Republic of China. The readers were jointly developed by Beijing Chinese Language College, Nanjing Normal University and Anhui Normal University. Serving as teaching aids for learners of Chinese, these readers make the general knowledge of Chinese culture, history and geography accessible to the young generation of overseas Chinese by means of either classroom delivery or self-study. These books are also for parents to help their children with the study. The previous versions of these readers were well received.

In recent years, with the rapid economic and social development in China and the rising of her international status, the world witnesses a phenomenal increase in learners of the Chinese language outside China, especially from non-Chinese ethnic groups. To meet the demand from overseas Chinese learners to better their knowledge about Chinese culture, and to foster cultural exchanges between China and the world, a revision of the above-mentioned readers has been decided by the Overseas Chinese Affairs Office of the State Council of the People's Republic of China. They assigned the Office of Chinese Language Council International to work out the new edition of Common Knowledge About Chinese Culture, Common Knowledge About Chinese History and Common Knowledge About Chinese Geography.

The revised version of Common Knowledge About Chinese Culture, Common Knowledge About Chinese History and Common Knowledge About Chinese Geography is intended to be a popular edition of learning aid for Chinese culture in a conversational style. These readers make Chinese culture, history and geography more accessible to all people. Based on the original Chinese-English version edited by the Overseas Chinese Affairs Office of the State Council of the People's Republic of China, the newly-revised version has kept its bilingual format, only broadening the foreign language coverage to German, French, Japanese, Korean, Russian, Thai, Spanish and Arabic.

The Office of Chinese Language Council International delegates the revision of Common Knowledge About Chinese Culture, Common Knowledge About Chinese History and Common Knowledge About Chinese Geography to Higher Education Press, who adds and subtracts parts of the original Chinese version with amendments to some data and illustrations. The bilingual versions of Chinese-English, Chinese-German and Chinese-Thai are developed by Higher Education Press. The versions of Chinese-French, Chinese-Japanese and Chinese-Korean are developed by Foreign Language Teaching and Research Press. The Chinese-Russian, Chinese-Spanish and Chinese-Arabic versions are done by Sinolingua. All revisions are meant to be innovative while maintaining the original focus of being accurate, instructive and practical. It is our sincere hope that this series of readers become windows for you to know more about China, and bridges leading you to the world of Chinese.

We would especially like to express our sincere appreciation to many experts, scholars and Chinese teachers both at home and abroad for their pertinent suggestions.

Developed under a tight schedule, the new editions might be blotted with oversights and inappropriateness. We sincerely welcome readers, especially those better versed in the relevant fields to contribute ideas for the correction and future revision of these books.

The Office of Chinese Language Council International
November, 2006

目 录
Contents

锦绣河山
Land of Charm and Beauty

中国七大古都
Seven Ancient Capitals of China

魅力城市
Enchanting Cities

中国之旅
Traveling Around China

附录 I Appendix I

附录 II Appendix II

中国概览

A General Survey of China

中国 的地理位置

China's Geographic Location in the World

中国位于欧亚大陆的东部，太平洋的西岸。

中国的陆上疆界长达2万多千米，拥有14个邻国，东邻朝鲜，东北部、北部和西北部与俄罗斯、蒙古国、哈萨克斯坦、吉尔吉斯斯坦、塔吉克斯坦相邻，西部和西南部毗邻阿富汗、巴基斯坦、印度、尼泊尔、不丹，南接越南、老挝、缅甸。

大陆海岸线北起中朝边界的鸭绿江口，南到中越边界的北仑河口，总长1.8万多千米。中国濒临渤海、黄海、东海、南海四大海域和台湾岛东面的太平洋。沿海分布5 000多个岛屿，台湾岛是中国的第一大岛。岛屿海岸线长1.4万千米。

China's Geographic Location in the World

China is located in the east of the Eurasian Continent, to the west of the Pacific Ocean.

China has a land boundary of more than 20 000 km, bordering 14 countries, with DPR Korea to the east; Russia, Mongolia, Kazakhstan, Kyrgyzstan and Tajikistan to the north, northeast and northwest; Afghanistan, Pakistan, India, Nepal and Bhutan to the west and southwest; and Vietnam, Laos and Myanmar to the South.

China's coastline extends from the north at the estuary of Yalu River on the Sino Korean border to the south at the estuary of Beilunhe River ("Song Ka Long" in Vietnamese) on the Sino-Vietnam border, with a total length of more than 18 000 km. China is flanked by the Bohai Sea, the Yellow Sea, the East and South China Seas, with the Pacific to the east. It has more than 5 000 islands along the coast, with the largest one being Taiwan Island. The total length of the coastline of China's islands is 14 000 km.

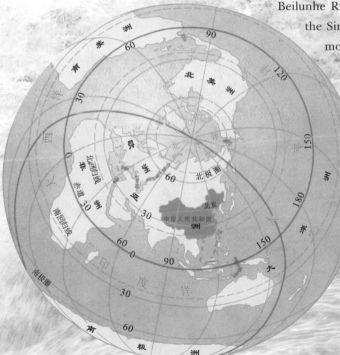

▶ 你知道吗？ Do you know?

同中国隔海相望的国家有日本、韩国、菲律宾、马来西亚、印度尼西亚和文莱。

China and the following countries face each other across the sea: Japan, the Republic of Korea, the Philippines, Malaysia, Indonesia and Brunei.

1. 中国的地形复杂多样
   China's diversified topography
2. 中国的地理位置
   China's geographic location in the world

1 | 2

3

中国的版图

China's Territory

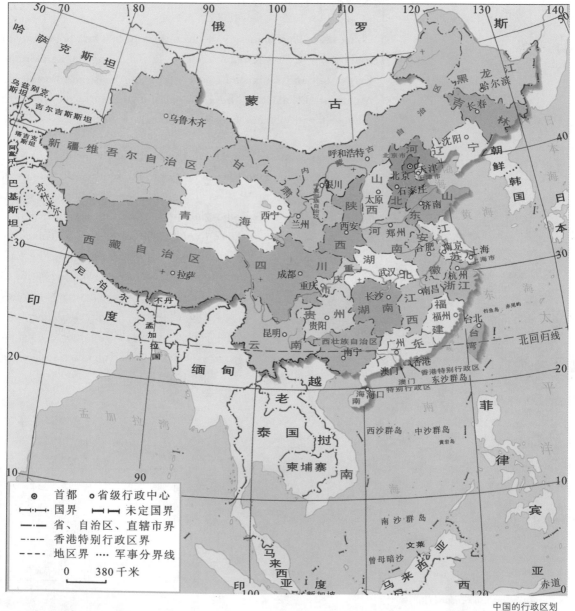

中国的行政区划
China's Administrative Divisions

中国行政区划简表
China's Administrative Divisions

序号 No.	全称 Full Name	简称 Abbreviation	行政中心 Administration Center
1	北京市 Beijing	京 Jing	北京 Beijing
2	天津市 Tianjin	津 Jin	天津 Tianjin
3	河北省 Hebei Province	冀 Ji	石家庄 Shijiazhuang
4	山西省 Shanxi Province	晋 Jin	太原 Taiyuan
5	内蒙古自治区 Inner Mongolia Autonomous Region	内蒙古 Inner Mongolia	呼和浩特 Hohhot
6	辽宁省 Liaoning Province	辽 Liao	沈阳 Shenyang
7	吉林省 Jilin Province	吉 Ji	长春 Changchun
8	黑龙江省 Heilongjiang Province	黑 Hei	哈尔滨 Harbin
9	上海市 Shanghai	沪 Hu	上海 Shanghai
10	江苏省 Jiangsu Province	苏 Su	南京 Nanjing
11	浙江省 Zhejiang Province	浙 Zhe	杭州 Hangzhou
12	福建省 Fujian Province	闽 Min	福州 Fuzhou
13	安徽省 Anhui Province	皖 Wan	合肥 Hefei
14	江西省 Jiangxi Province	赣 Gan	南昌 Nanchang
15	山东省 Shandong Province	鲁 Lu	济南 Jinan
16	河南省 Henan Province	豫 Yu	郑州 Zhengzhou
17	湖北省 Hubei Province	鄂 E	武汉 Wuhan
18	湖南省 Hunan Province	湘 Xiang	长沙 Changsha
19	广东省 Guangdong Province	粤 Yue	广州 Guangzhou
20	海南省 Hainan Province	琼 Qiong	海口 Haikou
21	广西壮族自治区 Guangxi Zhuang Autonomous Region	桂 Gui	南宁 Nanning
22	重庆市 Chongqing	渝 Yu	重庆 Chongqing
23	四川省 Sichuan Province	川或蜀 Chuan or Shu	成都 Chengdu
24	贵州省 Guizhou Province	贵或黔 Gui or Qian	贵阳 Guiyang
25	云南省 Yunnan Province	云或滇 Yun or Dian	昆明 Kunming
26	西藏自治区 Tibet Autonomous Region	藏 Zang	拉萨 Lhasa
27	陕西省 Shaanxi Province	陕或秦 Shaan or Qin	西安 Xi'an
28	甘肃省 Gansu Province	甘或陇 Gan or Long	兰州 Lanzhou
29	青海省 Qinghai Province	青 Qing	西宁 Xining
30	宁夏回族自治区 Ningxia Hui Autonomous Region	宁 Ning	银川 Yinchuan
31	新疆维吾尔自治区 Xinjiang Uygur Autonomous Region	新 Xin	乌鲁木齐 Urümqi
32	台湾省 Taiwan Province	台 Tai	台北 Taipei
33	香港特别行政区 Hong Kong Special Administrative Region	港 Gang	香港 Hong Kong
34	澳门特别行政区 Macao Special Administrative Region	澳 Ao	澳门 Macao

中国领土的最北端是黑龙江省漠河以北的黑龙江主航道中心线，最南端是南沙群岛的曾母暗沙。南北跨50个纬度左右，相距5 500千米。当东北进入隆冬季节的时候，南方的海南岛依然是一片夏季的景象。

中国领土的最东端是黑龙江和乌苏里江主航道中心线汇合处，最西端在新疆维吾尔自治区乌恰县西部的帕米尔高原上，东西跨经度60多度，相距5 000多千米。当东海之滨的渔民迎朝阳出海捕鱼的时候，帕米尔高原的牧民还在深夜中酣睡呢！

中国的陆地国土面积为960万平方千米，仅次于俄罗斯、加拿大，居世界第三位。另外，还拥有300万平方千米的海洋国土。

目前，中国有23个省、5个自治区、4个直辖市和两个特别行政区。首都是北京。

中国国土辽阔，资源丰富，江山多娇。中国是世界四大文明古国之一，中华民族在这块广阔的土地上，创造了光辉灿烂的东方文化。

China's **Territory**

The country stretches from north to south for about 50° in latitude, over a span of 5 500 km in distance, from the central line of the Heilongjiang River's main channel, north of Mohe county, to the Zengmu Reef of the Nansha Islands in the South China Sea. When the Northeast China hits the depth of winter, the Hainan Island in the south is still in its summer.

China's length spans for about 60° in longitude or more than 5 000 km in distance, from the junction of the central line of the Heilongjiang and Ussuri rivers in the east to the Pamir Highlands, west of Wuqia county, Xinjiang Uygur Autonomous Region in the far west. When fishermen living by the East China Sea sail out to work in the morning, herdsmen on the Pamir Highlands are still sound asleep at midnight.

China's land area is 9 600 000 km², ranking 3rd in the world after Russia and Canada. Besides, it also has a sea area of 3 000 000 km².

China has 23 provinces, 5 autonomous regions, 4 municipalities directly under the central government and 2 special administrative regions, with Beijing as its capital.

As one of the four great countries with ancient civilization, China has a vast territory, abundant resources and beautiful scenery. Chinese people have created glorious oriental culture on this vast land.

| 1 | 2 |

1. 帕米尔高原
   The Pamirs
2. 漠河的冬天
   Winter at Mohe

中国的人口

China's Population

中国是世界上人口数量最多的国家，截至 2000 年 11 月 1 日，全国总人口为 12.95 亿，2005 年 1 月 6 日是中国 "十三亿人口日"，今天中国人口已经超过 13 亿。中国人口约占世界总人口的 22% 左右。

中国的人口，地区分布不均匀。东部人口多，西部人口少；平原地区人口多，山地、高原地区人口少。

在中国城乡人口构成中，城镇人口比重小，乡村人口比重大。1949 年以来，中国非农业人口有计划地稳步增长，非农业人口增长的速度将会加快，占总人口的比重也将不断增加。

China's **Population**

China accounts for the largest population in the world. By Nov. 1, 2000, the national population had amounted to 1.295 billion. January 6th of 2005 was China's "1.3-billion population day". At present, China's population exceeds 1.3 billion. Chinese people now constitute about 22% of the world's population.

China's population is not evenly distributed across the country. The east of China has large population, while the west is sparsely populated. People abound in the plain areas, but are sparse in the mountainous and plateau regions.

The population in cities and towns contrasts sharply with that in the countryside—the former has small percentage in national population, while the latter constitutes a large proportion. Since 1949, China's non-rural population has increased steadily in a planned way. The growth of the non-rural population will accelerate even more and its percentage of the national population will also increase.

▶ 小资料 Data

2000 年，中国人口的平均寿命达 71.8 岁。

Chinese people's average life expectancy extended to 71.8 years in 2000.

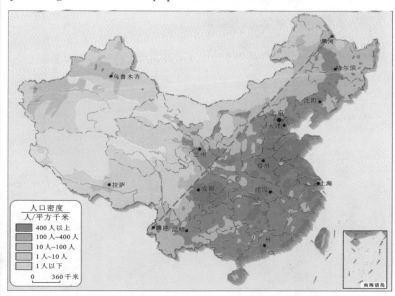

人口密度
人/平方千米
400 人以上
100 人~400 人
10 人~100 人
1 人~10 人
1 人以下
0   360 千米

1. 人们聚集在天安门广场，欢度国庆
   National Day celebration at Tian'anmen Square

1 | 2

2. 中国人口密度分布
   Distribution of China's Population

统一 的多民族大家庭

Unified Multi-ethnic Country

中国是一个统一的多民族国家，由汉、蒙古、回、藏、维吾尔、苗、彝、壮、布依、朝鲜、满等56个民族组成，实行民族平等的政策。

在各个民族中，汉族人口最多，约占全国总人口的91.59%。除汉族以外的55个民族统称为少数民族。第五次（截至2000年11月1日）人口普查结果显示少数民族总人口为10 643万，约占全国总人口的8.41%。

少数民族人口数量虽少，但地区分布很广，主要分布在西北、西南和东北等地。维吾尔族主要分布在新疆，是一个能歌善舞的民族；蒙古族主要分布于内蒙古高原，被称为"草原民族"；藏族主要分布在青藏高原，被称为"高原之鹰"；鄂伦春族分布在兴安岭山地，被称为"山岭上人"。

千百年来，中国各族人民在不同的自然和社会历史条件下，形成了不同特色的风俗习惯。

Unified **Multi-ethnic** Country

China is a unified multi-ethnic country, comprising 56 nationalities such as Han, Mongolian, Hui, Tibetan, Uygur, Miao, Yi, Zhuang, Buyi, Korean, and Manchu, etc. The policy that all of the nationalities are equal has become a national practice.

The Han people comprise the largest population among all of the nationalities, making up 91.59 percent of the country's total population. The other 55 nationalities are called ethnic minorities. The fifth national census (up to Nov. 1, 2000) shows the population of all of the minorities is 106 430 000, accounting for about 8.41% of the national population.

Although the ethnic minorities are small in population, they are widely dispersed across the country, mainly in the Northwest, Southwest and Northeast. The Uygur, a people good at dancing and singing, mainly live in the Xinjiang Uygur Autonomous Region. The Mongols, distributed on the Inner Mongolian Plateau, are called "people of grassland". The Tibetan people by and large live on the Qinghai-Tibet Plateau, known as "eagle of the plateau". The Oroqens inhabit the Xing'anling mountains, which earns them the name "people on the mountains".

For thousands of years, Chinese people of various nationalities experienced different natural, historical and social conditions, which formed their own distinct customs.

▶ 你知道吗? Do you know?

1. 苗族
   The Miao nationality
2. 傈僳族
   The Lisu nationality
3. 侗族
   The Dong nationality
4. 满族
   The Manchu nationality
5. 维吾尔族
   The Uygur nationality

1	3
	4
2	5

在中国，还有一些至今未被正式识别的民族，其人数共 74.9 万，占全国总人口的 0.066％。

Up to now there are still some ethnic groups which haven't been officially identified in China. This part of the population amounts to 749 000, i.e. 0.066% of the total national population.

中国的地形

China's Topography

中国的地形复杂多样：有低平宽广的平原，有起伏和缓的丘陵，有峰峦高耸的山地，有海拔较高、面积广大的高原，有周围高、中间低的盆地。

中国的地形，从总体上看，山地多，平地少。山地约占全国陆地面积的2/3以上，平地不足1/3。海拔在500米以上的地区，约占全国陆地面积的3/4（其中海拔在3 000米以上的占26%），在500米以下的占1/4。

中国地势，西高东低，呈三级阶梯状分布。第一级阶梯是青藏高原，海拔多在3 000～5 000米；第二阶梯是海拔在1 000～2 000米的内蒙古高原、黄土高原、云贵高原以及其间的塔里木、准噶尔、四川等盆地；第三级阶梯是大兴安岭、太行山、巫山、雪峰山之东的三大平原以及江南、东南低山丘陵，平原和丘陵海拔分别在200米和500米以下。

高山、高原都分布在大兴安岭—太行山—巫山—雪峰山一线以西，丘陵和平原主要分布在这一线以东。黄河、长江、珠江等主要河流发源于西部的高原、山区，顺着地势的倾斜，东流入海。

这种地形特点，一方面，有利于来自东南方向的暖湿海洋气流深入内地，对中国东部的气候、植被、土壤和水文产生影响；另一方面，使河流形成较大的多级落差，蕴藏有利于多级开发的丰富水力资源。

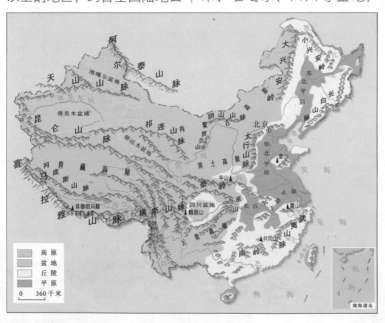

China's **Topography**

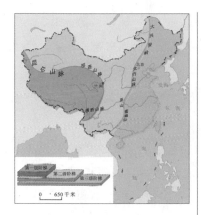

China has a varied and complicated topography. It has low, flat and wide plains, gently undulating hilly areas, mountainous regions with towering peaks, high and vast plateaus and bowl-shaped basins.

Generally speaking, China has more mountainous regions than flat ones. Mountainous areas make up about two-thirds of the country's land area, while the flats are less than one third. Regions higher than 500m cover about 3/4 of the national land area (among which regions higher than 3000m make up 26%), and regions lower than 500m account for 1/4.

China's land slopes from west to east and can be divided into three zones. The first zone is the Qinghai-Tibet Plateau, which has an average altitude around 3 000 to 5 000m. The second zone has a mean altitude ranging from 1 000 to 2 000m, including the Inner Mongolia, Loess and Yunnan-Guizhou plateaus, and the Tarim, Junggar, Sichuan and other basins which dot the plateaus. East of the mountains Da Xing'anling, Taihang, Wushan, and Snow Peak, the third zone consists of three big plains, and low hills around the lower reaches of the Yangtze River and the Southeast China. The plains are usually lower than 200m, and the low hills are less than 500m in altitude.

High mountains and plateaus are situated to the west of the line formed by the mountains Daxing'anling, Taihang, Wushan, and Snow Peak; and to the east of this line are hilly areas and plains. Some of China's major rivers, such as the Yellow River, the Yangtze River and the Zhujiang River, originating from the plateaus and mountains in the west, follow the slope of the topography, and flow east to the sea.

This characteristic yields two results. On the one hand, the sloping topography can make warm and humid sea air streams penetrate deep into the inland, impacting on east China's climate, plants, soil and hydrology. On the other hand, the sloping topography leads to the rivers' conspicuous drop in elevation step by step, producing rich hydraulic resources which can be exploited at various levels.

1. 中国地形分布示意图
   China's Topography
2. 中国地势三级阶梯示意图
   The Three-step Staircase of China's Topography

中国的气候

China's Climate

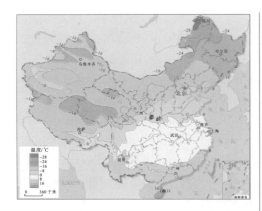

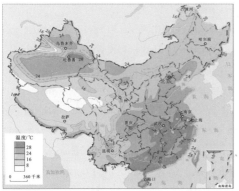

　　由于受到地理位置、大气环流、地势高低、人类活动等因素的影响，中国可以分为东部季风区、西北干旱半干旱区、青藏高寒区三大自然地理区。

　　中国的东部是世界上典型的季风气候区，大多数地方，冬季寒冷干燥，夏季高温多雨。

　　冬季，中国南北的气温差别较大。中国北方，冬季常常是千里冰封、万里雪飘的一片银装素裹的洁白世界。当东北的哈尔滨人冒着严寒参观"冰灯游园会"时，南方的广州却是百花盛开，春意盎然。

　　夏季，全国大部分地区普遍炎热，降水较多，雨热同季，给农业带来了极大好处。

　　全国的降水量，地区分布不均匀，从东南沿海向西北内陆逐渐减少。东南部地区降水较多，如台湾的火烧寮，年平均降水量多达6 557.8毫米；西北部地区降水少，新疆吐鲁番盆地中部，年平均降水量不到10毫米。

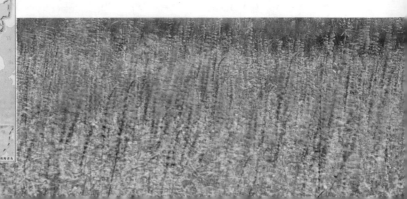

China's **Climate**

Due to factors like geographic position, atmospheric circulation, altitude and human activity, China can be divided into three climate zones, namely the east monsoon zone, the northwest dry and semi-dry zone and the Tibetan high and cold zone.

China's eastern part is a typical monsoon zone. Most areas in this part are cold and dry in winter, whereas hot and rainy in summer.

There is a big gap between the temperatures of north and south China in winter. In north China, the land is sometimes covered with snow and ice in winter. When people in Harbin, a city in northeast China, go on a visit to the ice lantern park in severe coldness, people in Guangzhou, a southern city, are enjoying a blossoming spring.

In summer, the majority of the country experiences high temperatures and plentiful rain. With high temperatures and plentiful rain in the same season, agriculture benefits a lot.

The precipitation is unevenly distributed across the country, decreasing from the southeast coast to northwest inland. Precipitation abounds in southeast areas but it is scarce in the northwest areas. For instance, Huoshaoliao in Taiwan has an annual rainfall of 6 557.8 mm, whereas in the central Turpan Depression, the annual rainfall is less than 10 mm.

1. 中国 1 月平均气温
   Average Temperature in January in China
2. 中国 7 月平均气温
   Average Temperature in July in China
3. 中国年降水量
   Average Annual Precipitation in China

1
2
3

▶ 你知道吗？ Do you know?

"季风" 可以简单地理解为风向随季节而发生显著变化的风。中国东部夏季盛行东南风，冬季盛行西北风。

每年的 6—7 月，江淮地区阴雨连绵，此时正是梅子成熟的季节，所以人们称这种雨为 "梅雨"。由于这一时期多雨阴湿，物品容易霉烂，又俗称 "霉雨"。

Monsoons can be simply defined as the wind that changes its direction conspicuously when the season changes. In east China, southeast wind is prevalent in summer, and northwest wind prevails in winter.

Every year from June to July, the drainage areas of the Yangtze and Huaihe Rivers are harassed by incessant rains. Since it is the time when plums ripen, people call this type of rain "plum rain". The rain is also called "mould rain", because things easily get mouldy in this rainy season.

▶ 小资料 Data

北京与纽约的纬度位置相近，但是，北京冬季比纽约冷，夏季比纽约热。7 月份与 1 月份的气温相比，北京相差 30.9℃，纽约相差 23.6℃。

Beijing is at about the same latitude as New York. However, Beijing is colder than New York in winter and hotter in summer. The difference in temperature between July and January in Beijing is 30.9 ℃, while it is 23.6℃ in New York.

中国的经济

China's Economy

中国自1978年实行改革开放的政策以来，经济获得了持续快速的发展。目前经济总量已位居世界前列。其中，粮食、棉花、肉类、布匹、钢、原煤、电视机等工农业产品的产量尤为突出；原子能、生物技术、计算机技术、航空航天技术等方面也已经达到或接近世界先进水平。

中国改革开放以后，从海外引进了大量的人才、资金和技术，大大加快了经济发展的步伐。预计到21世纪中叶，中国将基本上实现现代化，达到中等发达国家的水平。

中国是一个人口大国，按人口平均的经济水平还不高，仍然属于低收入国家，与发达国家相比，还存在较大的差距。

中国经济发展水平的地区差异较大，东部沿海地区比较发达，经济和科学技术发展水平较高，工业、农业、交通运输业和通讯业设施基础较好，西部地区相对落后。但是，从长远来看，西部地区资源丰富，有发展工农业的广阔空间。

中国正在进行西部大开发，以加快西部地区经济发展的步伐。

China's **Economy**

Since China adopted the Reform and Opening-up Policy in 1978, its economy has experienced a fast and steady development. At present, it is among the world's top economic powers. Its output of agricultural and industrial products such as crops, cotton, meat, cloth, steel, coal and TVs are outstanding, and its technologies of nuclear energy, biology, computers, aeronautics and astronautics have reached or almost caught up with the world's most advanced level.

Since the implementation of the Reform and Opening-up Policy, a large number of talents, vast amount of capital and technology have been imported from abroad, thus speeding up China's economic development. It is estimated that by the middle of the 21st century, China will have basically achieved modernization, coming up to the standard of the moderately developed countries.

However, in view of China's large population, its economic level is not yet high, and it still belongs to countries that have low per capita income. Compared with the developed countries, China

still has a long way to go.

Regional difference in China's economic development is considerably large. The coastal areas in the east are relatively more prosperous, having a higher level of economic and technological development, a better foundation of industry, agriculture, transportation and communication facilities. The western areas comparatively lag behind. But from a long-term point of view, the western areas have a vast space to develop its industry and agriculture, thanks to rich resources in these areas.

China is implementing Western Region Development strategy,

with a view to speed up the economic progress in this region.

▶ 小资料　Data

东部沿海地区有对外开放的深圳、珠海、汕头、厦门、海南5个经济特区以及大连、秦皇岛、天津、烟台、青岛、连云港、南通、上海、宁波、温州、福州、广州、湛江和北海14个沿海港口城市。

The eastern coastal areas have 5 open economic zones, namely Shenzhen, Zhuhai, Shantou, Xiamen and Hainan, and 14 coastal port cities, i.e. Dalian, Qinhuangdao, Tianjin, Yantai, Qingdao, Lianyungang, Nantong, Shanghai, Ningbo, Wenzhou, Fuzhou, Guangzhou, Zhanjiang and Beihai.

1. 北京王府井商业街
   Wangfujing Shopping Mall, Beijing
2. 上海集装箱码头
   Shanghai container terminal

中国的农业

China's Agriculture

中国是一个农业大国，同时也是世界上农业发展历史最悠久的国家之一，水稻等主要农作物都起源于中国。

秦岭淮河线，是南北地域分异的重要地理界线。

秦岭淮河线以北的北方，作物多为旱作，以小麦、玉米、高粱、大豆为主，偏南部可种植棉花、甘薯等。果木有苹果、梨、桃、杏、柿、核桃、板栗、枣、葡萄等。

秦岭淮河线以南的南方，全年都有作物生长，主要作物为水稻，一年二熟至三熟。南部还可栽培香蕉、菠萝、龙眼、荔枝、椰子等。

中国政府十分重视农业生产，不断加大农业投入，积极进行农田水利基本建设，从而提高了农业生产的现代化水平，使农业取得了辉煌的成就。最突出的表现是：中国仅依靠占世界不足 7% 的耕地，养活了占世界 22% 的人口。

▶ 你知道吗？ *Do you know?*

中国各种农产品的产量增长很快，谷物、肉类、棉花、油菜、花生、水果的总产量均居世界第一位。但是，由于人口数量多，人均占有的农产品数量较少。

The production of various crops in China has fast growth rate. The output of grains, meat, cotton, rape, peanuts and fruit rank first in the world. However, the output per capita is comparatively small due to its large population.

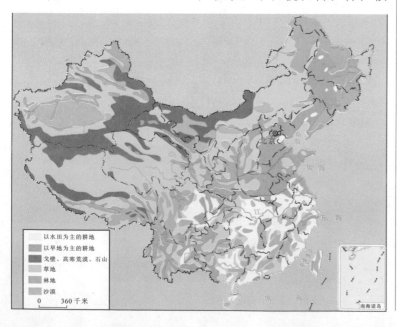

以水田为主的耕地
以旱地为主的耕地
戈壁、高寒荒漠、石山
草地
林地
沙漠

0   360千米

北京

黄河

江

东海

南海诸岛

China's **Agriculture**

China is a big agricultural country. It is also one of the countries with the longest history of agriculture development in the world. Crops like rice originated from China.

The Qinling Mountains and the Huaihe River serve as an important demarcation line of north-south boundary in China.

The northern region north to this line mainly grows dry crops like wheat, corn, Chinese sorghum and soybean. In the south of this region, cotton and sweet potatoes are planted. Fruits grown in this region include apples, pears, peaches, apricots, persimmons, walnuts, Chinese chestnuts, jujubes and grapes.

The southern region south to the line grows crops all year round. The staple crop is rice, which can be harvested two or three times in a year. The southern region also grows bananas, pineapples, longans, lychees, coconuts, etc.

The Chinese government attaches great significance to agriculture. It constantly increases investment in agriculture by actively building farmland irrigation and water conservation infrastructure. These efforts have led to China's improvement of agricultural modernization and great accomplishments in agriculture. This is particularly shown by the fact that China manages to feed 22% of world population with less than 7% of the world's cultivated land.

1. 中国的土地资源
   Land Resources in China
2. 云南的梯田
   Terrace in Yunnan Province

中国的工业

China's Industry

1949 年中华人民共和国成立以后，工业发展迅速，现在已建立了独立完整的现代化工业体系，拥有钢铁、化工、机械、纺织、电子、航空航天等所有的工业门类。

1949 年以前，中国的工业大部分都分布在沈阳、大连、天津、青岛、上海、广州等东部沿海城市，广大的中、西部地区，除武汉、重庆等少数城市外，工业水平都非常低。

1949 年以后，中国工业的地区分布发生了很大的变化，已形成了辽宁省中、南部地区的重工业基地；以北京—天津—唐山为中心的综合性工业基地；以上海—南京—杭州为中心的全国最大的综合性工业基地；珠江三角洲地区以广州、深圳为主的综合性工业基地。

China's Industry

Since the People's Republic of China was founded in 1949, China's industry has been developing quickly. Now an independent and comprehensive industrial system has been built up, which includes all industries, such as steel and iron, chemical engineering, mechanics, textiles, electronics, aeronautics and astronautics.

Before 1949, China's industry was mainly distributed in the coastal cities of the east, such as Shenyang, Dalian, Tianjin, Qingdao, Shanghai and Guangzhou. In the vast expanse of central and western China, the industry level was extremely low, except for a few cities like Wuhan and Chongqing.

1. 首钢集团
   A plant of Shougang Group

1 | 2

2. 深圳的加工厂
   A workshop in Shenzhen City

Since 1949, China's industrial layout has changed greatly. Now it has established a series key projects: a heavy industrial base in central and southern Liaoning Province, a comprehensive industrial base centered around Beijing, Tianjin and Tangshan, the nation's biggest comprehensive industrial base with Shanghai, Nanjing and Hangzhou as the centre, and comprehensive industrial base centered around Guangzhou and Shenzhen in the Zhujiang Delta area.

▶ 你知道吗？ Do you know?

中国是世界上最大的电视机、钢、水泥、原煤、化肥生产国。

China is the biggest manufacturer of TVs, steel, cement, coal and fertilizer.

资源与环境
Resources and Environment

矿产资源

Mineral Resources

中国幅员辽阔，矿产资源丰富。中国是世界上矿产资源总量丰富、矿产资源种类较齐全、配套程度较高的少数国家之一。截至 2002 年，已经探明的矿藏有 157 种，其中有些矿产为中国所独有。

煤炭作为中国的主要能源，其产量相当于世界煤炭总产量的 30%，居世界第一位。主要有开滦、大同、阳泉、淮南等煤矿。

中国石油、天然气资源比较丰富。陆上油田主要分布在东北、华北、西北等地，如大庆、胜利、辽河、克拉玛依、塔里木等油田。其中，大庆油田是中国最大的油田。此外，中国近海海域，也蕴藏着丰富的油气资源。

中国的有色金属储量丰富，品种繁多，其中钨、锡、锑、锌、钛、锂等金属的储量居世界首位。

虽然中国是资源大国，矿产资源总量居世界第三位，但由于人口众多，人均占有量仅列世界第 53 位。

Mineral Resources

China has a vast territory and rich mineral resources. It is among the few countries in the world that abound in mineral resources and varieties. By the year 2002, there were 157 confirmed minerals, some of which are found in China alone.

China's output of coal, the main energy resource in China, ranks first in the world, amounting to 30% of the world's total. The chief coal mines are located in Kailuan, Datong, Yangquan, Huainan, etc.

China is also rich in oil and natural gas. Oilfields on land are mainly distributed in Northeast, North and Northwest China, such as Daqing, Shengli, Liaohe, Karamay and Tarim oilfields. Among them, the Daqing Oilfield is the biggest one in China. Apart from these, the offshore area also abounds in oil and natural gas.

China abounds in various nonferrous metals, too. Its reserves of tungsten, tin, stibium, zinc, titanium, lithium and so on rank first in the world.

In terms of total reserves, China is rich in resources and takes third place in the world resource reservoir. But owing to its large population, the reserve per capita ranks only 53rd in the world.

动物 资源

Animal Resources

　　中国的动物资源非常丰富，种类非常多，约占全世界动物种类的 10％。其中鸟类 1 175 种，兽类 414 种，两栖类 196 种，爬行类 315 种，鱼类 2 000 多种。

　　有多种动物为中国所特有或主要分布在中国，如金丝猴、梅花鹿、丹顶鹤、大熊猫、扬子鳄、大鲵、野生双峰驼等。它们既是宝贵的自然资源，又是很有观赏价值的旅游资源。

丹顶鹤

　　丹顶鹤的寿命一般可达 50 ～ 60 年，所以又叫仙鹤。它体形优美，举止优雅，以喙、颈、腿"三长"著称，直立时可达 1 米多高。它身披洁白羽毛，裸露的朱红色头顶，好像一顶小红帽，因此得名。丹顶鹤是著名的观赏鸟，主要以鱼、虫、水草为食，夏季生活在黑龙江省的沼泽地，冬季飞往南方越冬。

　　全世界野生丹顶鹤的总数仅 1 200 只左右，而中国地区的丹顶鹤占全世界总数的 60% 左右，属于国家一类保护动物。

东北虎

　　东北虎，又称西伯利亚虎，起源于亚洲东北部，身体长约 1.6 ～ 2 米，是世界上体型最大的虎，堪称百兽之王。它的前额上有似"王"字的斑纹，一般在夜间活动。主要分布在中国的东北地区，是国家一类保护动物。

　　目前，野生东北虎在中国的分布已退至松花江南岸，集中在乌苏里江和图们江流域的中俄边境地带，数量很少。

麋鹿

麋鹿是中国特有的珍稀动物，因为它的角像鹿又不是鹿，头像马又不是马，身体像驴又不是驴，蹄子像牛又不是牛，所以又叫它"四不像"。因为它体型奇特，性情温驯，又非常稀少，是珍贵的观赏动物。

金丝猴

金丝猴又名"仰鼻猴"，是中国特有的珍贵动物，主要分布在四川、陕西、甘肃、湖北。毛色金黄，非常光亮，像金丝一样，所以叫金丝猴。体长 53 ~ 77 厘米，尾巴的长度与体长差不多。雄猴体大身强力壮，毛色鲜亮；雌猴较小，毛色略浅。

它们喜欢群居。食物以野

果、树叶、嫩枝芽为主，也吃苔藓植物。属于国家 类保护动物。

大熊猫

大熊猫是世界珍稀动物，是一种古老的动物，被动物学家称为"活化石"。分布在中国四川北部、陕西和甘肃南部，是国家一类保护动物。

大熊猫也叫"猫熊"，身体肥胖，形状像熊但要略小一些，尾巴短，眼睛周围、耳朵、前后肢和肩部是黑色，其余都是白色，性情温驯，动作笨拙，非常逗人喜爱。毛密而有光泽，耐寒。喜欢吃竹叶、竹笋。

中国曾经把大熊猫当作国礼送给友好国家，它成了"和平、友谊的使者"。现在世界野生生物基金会用大熊猫的图案作为该组织的会徽。

扬子鳄

扬子鳄是珍稀的淡水鳄类之一，是中国的特有品种，因产于扬子江而得名。一般休长两米多，头、躯干扁平，皮肤上覆盖大的鳞片，背面呈棕色，主要分布在安徽的宣城、广德、南陵等地。宣城建有扬子鳄自然保护区。

中国十分珍惜这些珍奇的野生动物，为了保护它们的生存坏境，建立了许多自然保护区，如四川的卧龙自然保护区、云南的西双版纳自然保护区、湖北的神农架自然保护区等，并且成立了专门的保护机构。

1. 东北虎
   Manchurian Tiger

1	2
	3

2. 金丝猴
   Golden Monkey

3. 大熊猫
   Giant Panda

Animal Resources

China has a great diversity of animals. The species in China are plentiful and account for 10% of the world's total. Among the species, there are 1 175 types of birds, 414 types of beasts, 196 species of amphibians, 315 types of reptiles and over 2 000 species of fish.

Some of these species are unique to China, or mainly live in China, such as the golden monkey, sika deer, red-crowned crane, giant panda, Chinese alligator, giant salamander and the wild two-humped camel. They are not only precious natural resources but also valuable tourist resources.

The Red-Crowned Crane

The red-crowned crane can live as long as 50 – 60 years, therefore it is also known as "the immortal crane". It has a graceful shape and elegant bearing. The red-crowned crane is famous for its long beak, neck and legs. When it stands erect, its height

reaches more than 1m. It has white plumage. With the bare vermillion top of the head, it seems to wear a small red hat, which explains why it gained the name. The red-crowned crane is a favorite of the tourists. They live on fish, insects and aquatic plants. In summer, they live in the swamps of Heilongjiang Province while in winter they fly south.

Altogether there are about 1 200 wild red-crowned cranes in the world. Those in China account for 60% of this number and are under State first-grade protection.

The Manchurian Tiger

The Manchurian tiger, also called Siberian tiger, originates from the northeast of Asia. Its body is about 1.6 – 2 m long. As the largest tiger in the world, it deserves the title of "the king of the animals". The pattern on its forehead resembles the Chinese

character "王 (wang, meaning the king)". The Manchurian tigers move around at night. They mainly live in the northeast of China and are granted State first-grade protection.

At present, wild Manchurian tigers are scarce, and have receded to the south bank of the Songhuajiang River, mainly at the Sino-Russian border area in the drainage area of the Ussuri and Tumen rivers.

David's Deer

David's deer is a rare animal that is unique in China. It has horns like a deer, a head like a horse, a body like a donkey, hoofs like an ox. So it is dubbed *Sibuxiang* (an animal of four-unlikeness). It is a precious animal for display because of its peculiar shape, tame temperament and rarity.

Golden Monkey

The golden monkey is also called the snub-nosed monkey. It is a rare animal unique to China. The golden monkeys are mainly dispersed in Sichuan, Shaanxi, Gansu and Hubei Provinces. Their name comes from their shiny golden hair, resembling thread of gold. Their bodies are about 53 – 72 cm long. The length of their tail is about the same as that of their body. The male golden monkey is big and strong with shining hair, whereas the female is relatively small with pale hair. They like living in groups and feed on wild fruits, leaves, twigs, and also bryophytes. They are granted the State first-grade protection.

Giant Panda

Giant pandas are rare animals in the world. They have a long history and are called "living fossils" by zoologists. They are mainly distributed over the north of Sichuan Province and the south of Shaanxi and Gansu Provinces. The giant panda is one of the first-grade animals under the state protection.

The giant panda is also called Maoxiong (meaning literally cat bear in Chinese). It is fat, resembling a bear but is a little bit smaller. Its tail is short. The hairs around its eyes and on its ears, limbs and shoulders are black, with the rest of the body being white. It has tame nature and clumsy movements, which make it look adorable. Its hairs are thick and shining, making it cold-resistant. It likes eating bamboo leaves and shoots.

China has sent some giant pandas as state presents to some countries of friendship. They have become "envoys of peace and friendship". Now the World Wildlife Fund (WWF) uses the giant panda as its logo.

Chinese Alligator
(Yangtze Alligator)

The Chinese alligator is one of the rarest freshwater alligators, and is peculiar to China. It is called the Yangtze alligator because its original habitat is the Yangtze River. It is usually more than two meters long. Its head and body are flat and it is covered with big squamae. Its back is brown. The Chinese alligators are mainly distributed in Xuancheng, Guangde and Nanling of Anhui Province. There is a natural reserve of Chinese alligators in Xuancheng.

All the above rare wild animals are treasures in China. To protect these animals' living environment, China has built many natural reserves, such as the Wolong Natural Reserve in Sichuan, the Xishuangbanna Natural Reserve in Yunnan, the Shennongjia Natural Reserve in Hubei and so on. Some special protective organizations have also been established for their sake.

丹顶鹤
Red-Crowned Crane

植物资源

Plant Resources

中国地理环境复杂，植物种类丰富多样。据统计，高等植物共 3 万多种，占世界植物种类的 1/10 左右。

中国众多的植物种类中，有各种各样的松树、终年常绿的柏树、姿态优美的杉树、清秀挺拔的竹子以及色彩缤纷的花卉等。

Plant Resources

China has a complicated geographical environment with a variety of plants. According to statistics, there are more than 30 000 species of higher plants, accounting for one-tenth of the world's total.

Among China's numerous plant species, there are various pine trees, evergreen cypresses, graceful China firs, delicate, tall and straight bamboos and colorful flowers, etc.

▶ 你知道吗？ Do you know?

闻名世界的三大"活化石"植物是水杉、银杏和银杉，它们在中国都有分布。

The three world-renowned "living fossil" plants are the metasequoia, the gingko and the Cathaya argyrophylla. They are all found in China.

▶ 小资料 Data

水杉是古老的稀有树种。过去，人们以为水杉在世界上早已绝迹。到了20世纪40年代，中国植物学家在四川省万县发现了水杉，成为当时国际植物学界的重大发现。

The metasequoia is a rare species with a long history. People used to believe metasequoia had become extinct. However, in 1940s, Chinese botanists found a metasequoia in Wan County, Sichuan Province. This was a monumental discovery in international botany circles at that time.

$\frac{1}{2}$ 3

1. 桦树林
   Birches
2. 银杏
   Gingko
3. 水杉
   Matasequoia

水资源

Water Resources

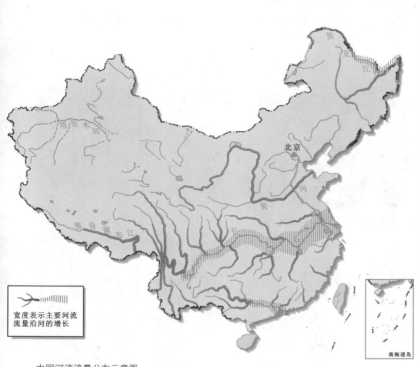

中国河流流量分布示意图
Distribution of Rivers in China

宽度表示主要河流流量沿河的增长

湖、太湖、巢湖等。另外，冰川面积也比较大，是重要的淡水资源。

中国河川径流虽然很丰富，但地区分布却很不均匀。水资源总的来说是东南多，西北少，由东南向西北递减。

中国各河径流量的大小相差悬殊。长江是中国最大的河流，长度为6 300千米，多年平均径流总量为9 755亿立方米，占全国径流总量的1/3以上，仅次于南美洲的亚马逊河和非洲的刚果河，居世界第3位。第二是珠江，多年平均径流总量为3 360亿立方米。雅鲁藏布江排第3位，多年平均径流总量为1 395.4亿立方米。黄河是中国第二大河，长度为5 500千米，但水量只排在第8位。

中国还有丰富的地下热水资源，全国露出地面的温泉就有2 600多处。

中国水资源总量位居世界前列。但人均拥有量却低于许多国家，仅相当于世界人均占有量的1/4。

中国江河湖泊众多，主要河流有长江、黄河、珠江、雅鲁藏布江、松花江等；主要湖泊有洞庭湖、鄱阳湖、洪泽

Water Resources

The total volume of water resources in China leads the world. But water per capita is only a quarter of the world average.

China abounds in rivers and lakes. The major ones are the Yangtze River, Yellow River, Pearl River, Yarlung Zangbo River and Songhua River. The major lakes include the Dongting Lake, Poyang Lake, Hongze Lake, Taihu Lake and Chaohu Lake. In addition, there is a large area of glaciers that are an important freshwater source.

China's water resources are unevenly distributed. Generally speaking, there is much more water in southeast than in northwest. The level of water resources descend from southeast to northwest.

There is great disparity between China's different rivers' runoff volumes. The Yangtze River is the largest in China with a length of 6 300 km. Its average runoff volume is about 975.5 billion m^3 annually. This amount is more than 1/3 of the country's total, ranking third place in the world, second only to the Amazon River in South America and the Congo River in Africa. The second one in China is the Pearl River. Its average runoff volume is 336 billion m^3 for many years. The third one is the Yarlung Zangbo River, with its average runoff amount reaching 139.54 billion m^3. The Yellow River is the second largest river in China, measuring 5 500 km long. But its runoff volume only ranks eighth in the country.

China also has rich subterranean hot water resources. There are more than 2 600 surface hot springs across the country.

> ▶ 小资料 Data
>
> 中国许多重要城市，如北京、沈阳、太原、西安等，供水水源主要为地下水。与地表水相比，它有着水量稳定、水质较好、水温低和可就地开采利用等优点。
>
> In China many major cities, such as Beijing, Shenyang, Taiyuan and Xi'an use underground water as their main water supply. Compared with surface water, underground water has advantages like stable quantity, good quality, low temperature and convenient for exploitation, etc.

环境保护

Environmental Protection

中国是一个发展中的大国，又处在工业化的过程中，环境问题比较突出，因此国家把环境保护列为一项基本国策。

近年来，中国政府采取了各种措施来加强环境治理。如建立了世界著名的生态工程"三北防护林工程"；大力发展和广泛建立自然保护区；颁布了《环境保护法》；加强环境保护的宣传和教育。目前，环境治理已取得了明显成效，大部分城市环境和农业生态环境得到了改善，工业污染防治能力也大大提高，环境保护已成为人人关心的话题，日益得到人们的重视。

Environmental Protection

China is a big developing country in the process of industrialization. Therefore, the environmental problem is comparatively prominent. The government has consequently taken environmental protection as one of its fundamental policies.

The government has taken various measures to strengthen environmental improvement in recent years, such as launching the world-famous ecological project "the shelter-forests in Northern, Northwestern and Northeastern China", setting up natural reserves, issuing Law on Environmental Protection, strengthening education on environmental protection, etc. Up to now, great achievements have

1. 湖北神农架自然保护区
   Shennongjia Natural Reserve, Hubei Province
2. 吉林长白山自然保护区
   Changbai Mountains Natural Reserve, Jilin Province

been made in environmental improvement. The environment in most cities and the agricultural ecological environment has been improved. The capability of preventing and controlling industrial pollution has been greatly enhanced. Environmental protection has become a hot topic, receiving increasingly more attention on the part of the whole nation.

四川卧龙自然保护区
Wolong Natural Reserve, Sichuan Province

交通与水利
Transportation and
Water Conservancy

铁路

Railways

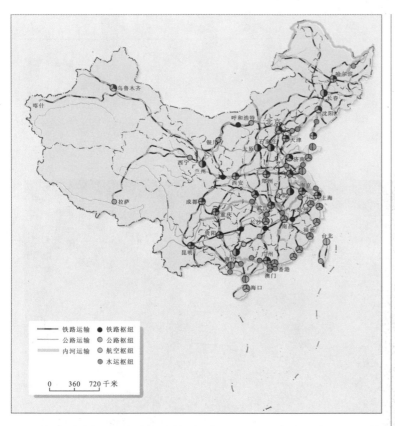

铁路是中国最重要的运输方式，到 2005 年底，铁路营运里程达 7 万多千米，居世界第三位。

中国铁路干线可以分为南北干线和东西干线两大组，在南北干线和东西干线的交叉或衔接处，形成了许多重要的铁路枢纽，如北京、上海、天津、重庆、哈尔滨、徐州、西安、武汉等。东西干线主要有京包—包兰线、陇海—兰新线、沪杭—浙赣—湘黔—贵昆线；南北干线主要有京哈—京广线、京沪线、京九线、焦柳线、宝成—成昆线等。这"三横"、"五纵"构成了中国铁路干线的主要骨架。

京广铁路北起北京，南到广州，穿过河北、河南、湖北、湖南、广东五省，全长 2 324 千米，是纵贯中国南北的交通大动脉，全线货运、客运都十分繁忙。

京沪铁路是纵贯中国东部地区的主要铁路干线，贯穿北京、天津、上海三个直辖市以及河北、山东、安徽、江苏四省，是首都北京通向华东地区的主要干线，全长 1 462 千米。京沪沿线经济繁荣，城镇密布。

京九铁路从北京到香港的九龙，是介于京广、京沪两条纵向干线之间的又一条南北大动脉，对增强首都北京与香港以及南北方向的联系具有重要意义。

陇海—兰新铁路，东起连云港，西至西北重镇兰州，长1 736千米，这段称陇海线；由兰州向西至乌鲁木齐，长1 904千米，这段称兰新线。兰新线现已向西延伸至阿拉山口，与哈萨克斯坦铁路相连，成为亚欧大陆桥的一个组成部分。陇海—兰新铁路是横贯中国东西的交通大动脉，对沟通东部与西部、沿海与内地、中国与欧洲的联系以及西部大开发等都

具有极其重要的意义。

青藏铁路，从青海西宁经格尔木到西藏拉萨，全长1 956千米，是世界上海拔最高的铁路。2006年7月1日，青藏铁路全线开通并试运营。青藏铁路的建成使西藏交通运输的落后面貌得到质的改善，为西藏今后经济可持续发展提供了可靠的保证。

▶ 小资料 Data

从1997年4月1日开始，中国在主要铁路干线上实行了五次大提速，现在1 500千米路程以内的两地可以做到"夕发朝至"。

Since April 1, 1997, China has sped up the running of trains on the main trunk railways for five times. Now, one can depart in the evening and arrive at the destination in the early morning, if the distance between the two places is within 1 500 km.

1. 中国的交通运输网
   China's Transportation Network
2. 北京西客站
   Beijing West Railway Station

1
2

Railways

Railways provide a vital transportation mode in China. By the end of 2005, there were 70 000 km of track in use. This length ranks third in the world.

China's trunk railway lines can be divided into two groups, namely south-north lines and east-west ones. There are many important hubs where south-north and east-west lines crisscross or join each other, such as Beijing, Shanghai, Tianjin, Chongqing, Harbin, Xuzhou, Xi'an and Wuhan. The east-west trunk lines mainly include the Beijing-Baotou and Baotou-Lanzhou line, Lianyungang-Lanzhou and Lanzhou-Urumqi line, Shanghai-Hangzhou, Hangzhou-Nanchang, Zhuzhou-Guiyang and Guizhou-Kunming line. The south-north trunk railways mainly include the Beijing-Harbin and Beijing-Guangzhou line, Beijing-Shanghai line, Beijing-Kowloon line, Jiaozuo-Liuzhou line, Baoji-Chengdu and Chengdu-Kunming line. These three east-west and five south-north lines form the basic framework of Chinese trunk railways.

The Beijing-Guangzhou line extends from Beijing in the north to Guangzhou in the south, running through Hebei, Henan, Hubei, Hunan and Guangdong Provinces. It covers 2 324 km and is the main artery of transportation from north to south, carrying heavy loads of goods and passengers.

The Beijing-Shanghai line is the major trunk line in eastern China, linking the cities of Beijing, Tianjin and Shanghai and

1. 上海的磁悬浮列车
   Magnetic Levitation
   Train in Shanghai
2. 穿过崇山峻岭的铁路
   A railway crossing the
   mountains

the four provinces of Hebei, Shandong, Anhui and Jiangsu. This line is the main route that connects Beijing with the East China with a total length of 1 462 km. Cities and towns cluster along this line, making this region the most prosperous area in China.

The Beijing-Kowloon line is another north-south main artery, situated between the two longitudinal lines—the Beijing-Guangzhou and Beijing-Shanghai lines. It bears great importance in strengthening the connection between the nation's capital and Hong Kong, as well as between the country's north and south areas.

The Longhai-Lanxin Railway has two parts. One part, called the Longhai Line, starts from Lianyungang in the east to Lanzhou in the northwest with a length of 1 736 km; the other part, namely the Lanxin Line,

is about 1 904 km long, and extends from Lanzhou westward to Urumqi in Xinjiang. Now, the Lanxin Line has further extended westward to the Ala Mountain Pass. Connecting to the Kazakhstan rail system, it has become a key component in the Eurasian continental bridge. The Longhai-Lanxin Railway, a transportation aorta traversing China from east to west, has an important role to play in connecting east and west, coastal areas and inland, as well as China and Europe, and also in

developing the western region of China.

The 1 956-km-long Qinghai-Tibet Railway, from Xining in Qinghai Province via Golmud to Lhasa in Tibet is the highest railway in the world. On July 1st 2006, this railway was put into use. The success in building the Qinghai-Tibet Railway marks a fundamental change of Tibet's transportation and guarantees the sustainable development of Tibet's economy in the future.

公路

Roads

　　中华人民共和国成立以后，公路建设发展迅速，公路运输网已遍布全国各地，实现了"县县通公路"。到 2005 年底，公路通车里程已达 193.05 万多千米。

　　中国从 20 世纪 80 年代后期开始建设高速公路，到 2000 年底，中国大陆的高速公路总长度达 2.7 万千米。北京、上海、天津、沈阳、大连、武汉、南京、广州、深圳等主要城市都开通了高速公路。

Roads

Since the founding of the People's Republic of China in 1949, road construction has developed rapidly so that the transportation network has spread all over the country and every county has been connected by road. By the end of 2005, more than 1.9305 million km of roads had been put into use.

From the late 1980s, when expressways began to be constructed, to the end of 2000, a total of 27 000 km of expressways had been completed. Many of the major cities like Beijing, Shanghai, Tianjin, Shenyang, Dalian, Wuhan, Nanjing, Guangzhou and Shenzhen all have their own expressway networks.

1. 上海杨浦大桥
   Yangpu Bridge, Shanghai
2. 上海高速公路
   Expressway in Shanghai
3. 北京的立交桥
   Cloverleaf junction in Beijing

航空

Aviation

航空已成为中国重要的交通运输方式，到 2000 年底，国内民用航线已达 1 000 多条，主要城市之间都可通航，人们乘飞机出行已司空见惯。国际航线有 120 多条，通往世界各地的许多城市，北京、上海、广州、香港等是重要的国际航空港。

1. 北京首都机场
   Beijing Capital International Airport
2. 国航客机
   A passenger plane of Air Chia
3. 北京首都机场新旅客航站效果图
   A rendering of the new terminals of
   Beijing Capital International Airport

1 | 2
  | 3

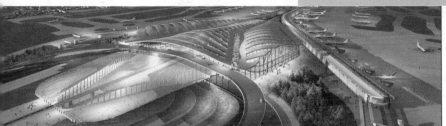

Aviation

Air transport is now an important mode of travel. By the end of 2000, the number of civil air routes in China had exceeded 1 000. All major cities are connected by airlines. It has become very common for people to travel by plane. There are over 120 international airlines to various cities all over the world. Beijing, Shanghai, Guangzhou and Hong Kong are among the most important international airports.

45

水运

Water Transportation

中国水运的发展历史十分悠久，远在商代就有了帆船。隋朝大运河的开通，为南北水上运输提供了极大的便利。明朝郑和7次下西洋，远及非洲东部沿海。

中国河流众多，海岸线漫长，水运条件优越。长江是中国最重要的内河航运大动脉。其干流从四川宜宾到入海口，全长2 813千米，全年可以通航，重庆、武汉、南京是长江沿岸重要的港口城市。珠江、松花江、黑龙江、淮河以及京杭运河也有一定的通航价值。

中国海运条件优越，拥有许多港口，如上海、大连、秦皇岛、天津、青岛、宁波、厦门、广州等。远洋船舶可达世界150多个国家和地区。

Water Transportation

China's water transport has a long history. Early in the Shang Dynasty (1600 – 1046 BC) , there were sailing boats. The Great Canal of the Sui Dynasty (581 – 618 AD) provided great convenience for south-north water transport. In the Ming Dynasty (1368 – 1644 AD), Zheng He (1371 – 1433 AD) navigated across the seas seven times and reached the eastern coast of Africa in one of his voyages.

China has numerous rivers and a long coastline, which contributes to its advantageous water transportation. The Yangtze River is the most important inland shipping artery. Its main stream, from Yibin in Sichuan Province to the sea, has a total length of 2 813 km and is navigable all year round. Chongqing, Wuhan and Nanjing are important ports along the river. The Pearl River, the Songhua River, the Heilongjiang River, the Huaihe River and the Beijing-Hangzhou Canal are also of considerable navigational value.

China has favorable conditions for sea transportation, with numerous harbors in such cities as Shanghai, Dalian, Qinhuangdao, Tianjin, Qingdao, Ningbo, Xiamen, Guangzhou and so on. There are ocean-going ships sailing from these ports to more than 150 countries and regions all over the world.

1. 深圳蛇口港码头
   Shekou Harbor, Shenzhen
2. 上海浦东航运货轮
   Freighter in Pudong Harbor, Shanghai
3. 上海浦东码头
   Pudong Harbor, Shanghai

三峡工程

The Three Gorges Project

三峡工程是一项综合治理长江和开发长江水能资源的宏大工程，是中国也是世界最大的水利枢纽工程，具有防洪、发电、航运等综合功能。

大坝坝址位于湖北省宜昌市三斗坪，在已建成的葛洲坝水利枢纽上游的40千米处。水库正常蓄水位175米，总库容393亿立方米。三峡工程可以从根本上解除长江中下游的水患威胁。

三峡工程相当于10座200万千瓦的大型火力发电站，可以缓解华中和华东等地区的能源紧张状况。

三峡工程可以改善长江上游航道的通航条件。2011年工程建成后，万吨级船队可以直达重庆，航运成本可降低35％，从而加强西南与其他地区的联系。

▶ 你知道吗？ Do you know?

长江三峡大坝是"世界第一坝"，坝长2 309米。它就像横跨长江的"水上长城"，是一处吸引游客的新景观。

The Three Gorges Dam of the Yangtze River is the biggest dam in the world. It is 2 309 m long and looks like a Great Wall on the water, attracting tourists as a new landscape.

The **Three Gorges** Project

The Three Gorges Project is a grand engineering to harness the Yangtze River and exploit its hydropower potential. It is the largest key water conservancy project in the world. It has comprehensive functions of preventing floods, generating electricity and facilitating shipping.

The dam is located at Sandouping in Yichang City, Hubei Province, 40 km upstream from the existing Gezhouba water conservancy hub. The reservoir's normal storage level is 175 m, and it can hold water of 39.3 billion m^3. The Three Gorges Project can fundamentally relieve the flood threats of the middle and lower reaches of the Yangtze River.

The capacity of the Three Gorges Project is equivalent to ten 2 million kw thermal power stations, and thus can ease the power shortage in Central and East China.

It can also improve the navigational condition of the upper reaches of the Yangtze River. After its completion, 10 000-ton ships can reach Chongqing directly, reducing the current shipping costs by 35%. The link between the southwest and other regions will consequently be strengthened by the project.

▶ 小资料   Data

三峡大坝高185米，电站装机总容量 1 820 万千瓦，年平均发电量约 847 亿千瓦时，是目前世界上最大的水电站。三峡工程 1994 年 12 月正式开工，总工期预计约 17 年，是一项跨世纪的工程。

The dam of the Three Gorges is 185 m high. Its hydropower station has a capacity of 18.2 million kw, with an annual generating capability of 84.7 billion kw. Now it is the largest hydropower station in the world. The Three Gorges Project began in December of 1994 and was scheduled for completion in 17 years, and hence the name "trans-century project".

1. 三峡大坝
   The dam of the Three Gorges
2. 三峡大坝
   The dam of the Three Gorges

小浪底 水利枢纽工程

The Xiaolangdi Key Water Control Project

小浪底位于河南洛阳以北40千米的黄河干流上，处在控制黄河下游泥沙的关键部位。小浪底水利枢纽工程是一座以防洪、减少泥沙淤积为主，兼顾灌溉、供水和发电等综合效益的特大型控制工程。

▶ 你知道吗？ Do you know?

小浪底水利枢纽工程建成后，使黄河下游的防洪标准从60年一遇提高到千年一遇。

Since the completion of the Xiaolangdi Key Water Control Project, the standard of the flood control over the lower reaches of the Yellow River has been improved, from being able to tackle the catastrophic flood occurring in every 60 years to that of every 1000 years.

The **Xiaolangdi**
Key Water Control Project

Xiaolangdi is located on the main stream of the Yellow River 40 km north of Luoyang, Henan Province, at the critical location in controlling the mud and sand of the lower Yellow River. The Xiaolangdi Key Water Control Project is an exceptionally large-scale construction project aiming to control floods, reduce sand and mud deposits, and also pursue other comprehensive benefits like irrigation, supplying water and generating electricity.

1. 小浪底水库
   Xiaolangdi Reservoir
2. 小浪底水库
   Xiaolangdi Reservoir

南水北调

Water Diversion from South to North

1
2

1. 南水北调路线示意图
   A sketch Map of Water Diversion from South to North
2. 南方水资源丰富
   Abundant water resources in South China

中国的水资源，地区分布不均匀。总的来说南方多，北方少；东部多，西部少。随着人口的增加和经济的发展，北方缺水的情况日益严重，解决这一问题的办法之一就是跨流域调水，即南水北调。

南水北调工程包括东、中、西三条线路。

东线从长江下游提水，沿京杭运河北送，可为华北平原东部补水。渠长1 150千米，每年引水量300亿立方米。东线不需要开挖新干渠，可利用已建成的江都、淮安抽水站设施和京杭运河，并且沿途有许多湖泊可作为调节水库。

中线是从长江中游及其主要支流汉江引水到华北平原西部。全长1 000多千米，每年引水量300亿立方米，其优点是引水量大，还可利用落差兴建水力发电站。

西线从长江上游引水到黄河上游，主要为黄河上中游及西北地区补水。西线调水都在高山峡谷地区进行，海拔高，施工材料缺乏，交通不便，投资巨大。

三条线路可以互相配合，根据国家各阶段经济发展的需要和财力的情况分期开发。近期会实施东、中线方案，西线是远景设想。

Water Diversion from South to North

Water resources in China are unevenly distributed. Generally speaking, the south is rich in water while the north is short of this resource; and the east is rich in water whereas the west lacks it. With the increase of population and rapid economic development, the problem of water shortage in the north is getting even more serious. One solution is to divert water from one drainage area to another, namely, from south to north.

The project of water diversion from south to north includes three lines—the east, middle, and west lines.

The east line will carry water from the lower reaches of the Yangtze River northward along the Beijing-Hangzhou Canal to the North China Plain. It is about 1 150 km, diverting 30 billion m^3 of water annually. There is no need to dig new channels along the east line. The facilities of the established Jiangdu and Huai'an pumping stations and the Beijing-Hangzhou Canal can be used to divert the water, and many

lakes along the line can serve as reservoirs for water regulation.

The middle line will draw water from the middle of the Yangtze River and its main tributary, the Hanjiang River, to the western side of the North China Plain. It is over 1 000 km long and could divert 30 billion m³ of water annually. It can not only divert a large volume of water but also

make use of the drop in altitude to build hydropower plants.

The west line will channel water from the upper reaches of the Yangtze River to the upper Yellow River to supply water for the upper and middle reaches of the latter and the northwestern regions. The west line will have to pass through mountains and gorges at high altitudes. Due to

the lack of construction materials and inconvenient transportation, this project will entail great efforts and investment.

The three lines can support one another and be developed by several stages according to national economic development and the existing financial capacity. In the near future, the east and middle lines will be constructed, while the west line is for a long-term plan.

1. 南水北调工程现场
   A location of Water Diversion project from South to North
2. 北方水资源贫乏
   Shortage of water in North China

1
2

锦绣河山
Land of Charm and Beauty

喜马拉雅山

The Himalayas

高峰有 40 座。其中位于中国与尼泊尔边界上的主峰珠穆朗玛峰海拔 8 844.43 米，是世界第一高峰，如同一座美丽的金字塔雄踞在喜马拉雅山的中段，素有"地球第三极"之称。

喜马拉雅山是地球上最年轻的山脉，因为它真正成为雄伟的山体仅有几十万年的历史，而且现在还在不断增高呢！

喜马拉雅山脉位于青藏高原的南缘，西起帕米尔高原，东到雅鲁藏布江大拐弯处，东西长 2 450 千米，南北宽 200 ~ 300 千米，平均海拔 6 200 米。

喜马拉雅山脉是世界上最雄伟高大的山脉，由数条大致平行的支脉组成，由北而南依次为大喜马拉雅山、小喜马拉雅山及西瓦利克山等。主脉大喜马拉雅山海拔 7 000 米以上的

The **Himalayas**

The Himalayas, situated at the south edge of the Qinghai-Tibet Plateau, range from the Pamir Plateau in the west to the great turning point of the Yarlung Zangbo River in the east. The mountains span over 2 450 km long from east to west, and 200 — 300 km wide from south to north, with an average altitude of 6 200 m.

The Himalayas, the most imposing and the highest mountain range in the world, are made up of several roughly parallel branch ranges. From north to south, they are the Big Himalayas, Small Himalayas, Siwalik Hills, etc. The Big Himalayas, main branch range of the Himalayas, boasts 40 peaks over 7 000 m high. Mount Qomolangma, at an altitude of 8 844.43 m, is the highest mount in the world. Located on the border of China and Nepal, it dominates the middle of the Himalayas like a majestic pyramid and is called the Third Pole of the world.

Emerged only several hundred thousand years ago, the Himalayas are the youngest mountains on the earth. Nowadays they are still growing!

▶ 你知道吗？ Do you know?

藏语中"喜马拉雅"是"冰雪之乡"的意思。7 000 米以上的高峰，山顶终年被积雪覆盖，冰川广布。

The Himalayas in the Tibetan language means "land of snow". All the peaks over 7 000 m are snow-capped all year round and glaciers can be found everywhere.

1. 珠穆朗玛峰
   Mount Qomolangma
1
2. 积雪覆盖的喜马拉雅山
2
   Snow-capped Himalayas

秦岭

The Qinling Mountains

秦岭山脉全长 1 500 千米，南北宽数十千米至二三百千米，气势磅礴，蔚为壮观。狭义的秦岭是指秦岭山脉中段，位于陕西省中部的一部分。

秦岭的最高峰是太白山，海拔 3 767 米，自古就是一座中华名山，"太白积雪六月天"是著名的长安八景之一。另一高峰华山海拔虽不过 2 000 多米，但山势险要，有"自古华山一条路"和"奇险天下第一山"之说。巨大的花岗岩体组成的五个峻峭山峰（东峰、西峰、南峰、北峰和中峰），像一朵五瓣的梅花绽开在山顶上，景色奇丽。

秦岭好像一堵挡风的高墙，横卧在中国的腹部。冬季，它

阻挡凛冽的西北风南下，使南方受寒潮影响减弱；夏季，它阻截了东南风带来的水汽，使北方降水大为减少。因此，秦岭山脉是中国南方和北方的天然分界线，也是长江、黄河两大水系的分水岭。

The **Qinling** Mountains

The Qinling Mountains span over 1 500 km long, and ten to two or three hundred thousand km wide from south to north. They are majestic and grandiose. The Qinling Mountains, in the narrow sense, refer to the middle section of the Qinling Range, a portion of the very mountain in central Shaanxi Province.

Mount Taibai, at an elevation of 3 767 m, is the highest peak of the Qinling Mountains. It has been a famous mount since ancient times. Snow-capped Taibai Peak in June is one of the eight renowned Chang'an (today's Xi'an) sights. Another high mountain in Qinling, Mount Huashan, though only about 2 000 m high, is very precipitous. Hence comes the famous saying, "there is no way to Mount Huashan except a precipitous path" and "the steepest mount in China". The five peaks, namely the East Peak, West Peak, South Peak, North Peak and Middle Peak, stand like a five-petal plum flower in full blossom, adding unique and charming scenery to Mount Huashan.

The Qinling Mountains stand like a huge wall blocking the wind in the hinterland of China. In winter, they stop the northwest wind from blowing southward, reducing the cold wave's influence on the south of China; in summer, they intercept the vapor brought by the southeast wind, reducing precipitation in the north areas. Therefore, the Qinling Mountains serve as a natural dividing line between the south and north of China, and also the watershed between the drainage areas of the Yangtze River and the Yellow River.

1. 太白山
   Mount Taibai
2. 华山
   Mount Huashan

2
1

长白山

The Changbai Mountains

长白山位于吉林省东南部，海拔 2 500 米以上的山峰有 16 座。

长白山天池是因火山口积水而形成的湖泊，池水清澈如镜，周围被峭壁山峰环绕，湖山相映，景色优美。

长白山是一座自然资源的大宝库。

从山脚到峰顶气候变化万千，景色十分壮观。

人们经常提到的"东北三宝"——人参、貂皮、鹿茸就产于此地。

The **Changbai** Mountains

The Changbai Mountains are located in the southeast part of Jilin Province, with 16 peaks over 2 500 m high.

The Heavenly Pond is formed by water accumulated in a crater. Encircled by precipitous mountains, the pond is as clear as a mirror. The pond offers a pleasing scene with its shimmering water against the green mountains.

The Changbai Mountains are a great treasure house of natural resources. The mountain area is the original producer of the well-known "three treasures of the Northeast" i.e. ginseng, mink and pilose antler.

1	2	4
3		5

1. 鹿茸
   Pilose antler
2. 人参
   Ginseng
3. 长白山天池
   The Heavenly Pond
4. 紫貂
   Sable
5. 长白山雪景
   Snow-capped Changbai Moutains

天山

The Tianshan Mountains

　　天山山脉全长 2 500 千米，分为西天山、中天山和东天山三部分。西天山在哈萨克斯坦和吉尔吉斯斯坦境内，东天山和中天山横贯中国新疆中部。

　　天山是新疆一条重要的自然地理分界线，天山南北的气候、水文动植物分布以及自然旅游景观具有明显的差异。它也是全国最大的现代冰川分布区，冰川融水成为新疆重要的河流补给来源。

　　天山景色秀丽。举目远望，只见山顶上白雪皑皑，冰川蜿蜒；山腰森林片片，绿草如茵；山脚下流水淙淙，一块块绿洲如花似锦。雄伟壮丽的天山是新疆维吾尔自治区重要的牧业生产基地之一。

1. 天山牧场
   A pasture on Tianshan Mountains
2. 天山雪景
   Snow-capped Tianshan Mountains

1 | 2

The **Tianshan** Mountains

The Range of Tianshan Mountains, with a total length of 2 500 km, includes the West Tianshan Mountains, Middle Tianshan

Mountains and East Tianshan Mountains. The West Tianshan Mountains is located within Kazakhstan and Kyrgyzstan. The East Tianshan Mountains and the Middle Tianshan Mountains span the central Xinjiang Uygur Autonomous Region in China.

The Tianshan Mountains are a natural geographic line of demarcation. There is a striking difference between the north and the south mountains in climate, hydrology, plants, animals and landscapes. And the nation's largest distribution area of modern glaciers are here. The melted glacier water supplies a major part of the source of many rivers in Xinjiang.

The Tianshan Mountains offer graceful scenery. Seen from afar, they are covered by a vast expanse of snow and by winding glaciers on the top; green trees and grass thrive halfway up the mountains; tinkling streams and beautiful oases provide a picturesque touch at the foot of the mountain. The grandiose Tianshan area is one of the bases of animal husbandry in the Xinjiang Uygur Autonomous Region.

昆仑山

The Kunlun Mountains

昆仑山西起帕米尔高原，东经青海省到四川省西北部，横贯新疆和西藏之间，全长 2 500 千米，它像一条长龙横卧在中国的西部，有"亚洲脊柱"之称。

昆仑山由东、中、西昆仑三部分组成。东昆仑像一只鸟爪一样分出南、中、北三支脉，属于南支的巴颜喀拉山是长江和黄河的分水岭。

昆仑山海拔多在 5 000 米以上，许多高峰超过 7 000 米。每年夏天山顶积雪开始融化，汇成一股股清澈的溪流，滋润着西北干旱的土地，补充长江和黄河的水源。

巍巍昆仑山
The Kunlun Mountains

The **Kunlun** Mountains

The Kunlun Mountains extend from the Pamirs in the west to the northwest of Sichuan Province, passing through Qinghai Province and traversing between Xinjiang and Tibet. Over 2 500 km long, they crouch like a huge dragon in the west of China, and hence the name "Spine of Asia".

The Kunlun Mountains comprise the East, Middle and West Kunlun Mountains. The southern, middle and northern branch ranges of East Kunlun Mountains spread like the claw of a bird. The Bayakala Mountain, belonging to the southern branch, is the watershed of the Yangtze and Yellow rivers.

Most of the peaks in the Kunlun range are over 5 000 m high, and some of them exceed 7 000 m. Every summer, the snow on the top of the mountains begins to melt, forming streams that moisten the dry land in the Northwest China and supplement the sources of the Yangtze and Yellow rivers.

▶ 小资料 Data

昆仑山气候寒冷，冰峰雪岭连绵不断，是中国冰川最多的山，高峰慕士塔格山有"冰川之父"的称号。众多的冰川如条条玉龙盘旋于山谷中，冰塔林、冰瀑布、冰裂缝琳琅满目。丰富的冰川与积雪成为许多江河的源泉。

The Kunlun Mountains are characterized by freezing weather. There are rolling ice-capped peaks and the largest number of glaciers in China. The Muztag Ata Mountain is reputed to be"the father of glaciers". Numerous glaciers are entrenched in valleys like jade dragons. Seracs, icy waterfalls and ice cracks can be found everywhere. A lot of glaciers and the accumulated snow become the sources of many rivers.

青藏 高原

The Qinghai-Tibet Plateau

青藏高原位于中国西南部，面积约230万平方千米，平均海拔4 000米以上，被称为"世界屋脊"，是中国的第一大高原。

青藏高原是典型的山地型高原。从北到南主要有祁连山、昆仑山、唐古拉山、冈底斯山以及喜马拉雅山等高大山脉。世界最高峰——珠穆朗玛峰就是喜马拉雅山的主峰。

青藏高原气温低，雪山连绵，形成了大面积的高山冰川，被称为"固体水库"。冰雪融水不仅是亚洲许多著名大河的发源地，也是中国内陆干旱地区重要的灌溉水源。

青藏高原是中国重要的天然牧场，高原上的草并不高，但因光照充足，光合作用旺盛，营养价值极高。每年夏秋季节，草原上牛羊成群，除了放牧的牦牛、藏山羊、藏绵羊和犏牛外，还有成群的黄羊、羚羊、野牛、野驴等野生动物。

The Qinghai-Tibet Plateau

Located in the southwest of China, the Qinghai-Tibet Plateau has an area of about 2.3 million km² and an average altitude of over 4 000 m. It is reputed as the "roof of the world" and is the biggest plateau in China.

The Qinghai-Tibet Plateau is a typical mountainous plateau. From north to south, it mainly comprises the Qilian Mountains, the Kunlun Mountains, the Tanggula Mountains, the Gandise Mountains, and the Himalayas. Mount Qomolangma, the highest mount in the world, is the main peak of the Himalayas.

The Qinghai-Tibet Plateau has a low temperature, undulating snow mountains and a large area of glaciers, so it is called a solid water reservoir. The melted ice and snow is not only the source of many famous Asian rivers, but is also the irrigating source for the arid region in inland China.

The plateau is an important natural pasture in China. The grass growing there is not tall, but is full of nutrition, owing to the rich sunshine and active photosynthesis. Every summer and fall, herds of cows and sheep graze there. Apart from grazing yaks, Tibetan goats, Tibetan sheep and *pian niu* (offspring of a bull and a female yak), there are herds of Mongolian gazelle, antelopes, wild oxen, Asiatic wild asses, and many other wild animals.

1. 俯瞰祁连山
   A bird's-eye view of the Qilian Mountains
2. 高原之舟——牦牛
   Ships on the plateau—Yaks

1 | 2

内蒙古 高原

The Inner Mongolian Plateau

内蒙古高原位于中国北部，面积约 100 万平方千米，平均海拔 1 000 米以上，是中国的第二大高原。

内蒙古高原开阔坦荡，地面起伏和缓。从飞机上俯视高原就像烟波浩瀚的大海。高原上既有碧野千里的草原，也有沙浪滚滚的沙漠，是中国天然牧场和沙漠分布地区之一。

内蒙古高原气候十分干燥，沙漠分布面积占全国沙漠总面积的 1/3 以上。较大的沙漠有巴丹吉林沙漠、腾格里沙漠、乌兰布和沙漠和库布齐沙漠等。

黄河流经内蒙古高原中部时，河谷较宽展，泥沙在此堆积，成为肥沃的冲积平原，这就是被人们称为"塞上江南"的河套平原。

内蒙古高原是中国著名的天然草场。"天苍苍，野茫茫，风吹草低见牛羊"，曾是草原的真实写照。但由于过度放牧等原因，导致草场退化，出现了荒漠化的现象。所以，中国正在实施的西部大开发战略把改善生态环境作为重要举措之一。

The **Inner Mongolian** Plateau

With an area of about one million km² and an altitude of more than 1 000 m, the Inner Mongolian Plateau is located in the north of China and is the second largest plateau in the country.

The Inner Mongolian Plateau is vast, with a moderately undulating surface. Seen from a plane, it looks like an immense sea. The plateau has not only vast green pastures, but also deserts of billowing sand. It is one of the areas where natural pasture and desert are found together.

The Inner Mongolian Plateau has very dry weather, as more than one-third of China's deserts are located there. Some big deserts on the plateau include the Badain Jaran Desert, the Tengger Desert, the Ulan Buh Desert and the Hobq Desert, etc.

As the Yellow River passes through the central Inner Mongolian Plateau, the river valley expands and sand accumulates to form a fertile alluvial plain. This is the Hetao Plain which is called "Jiangnan (areas south of the lower reaches of the Yangtze River) beyond the Great Wall".

The Inner Mongolian Plateau is the famous natural grassland in China. The verse "under the boundless sky is vast grassland, flocks and herds are gazing in the field ..." presents a vivid picture of the region in the remote past. Due to excessive grazing, the grassland has degencrated into desert in many places. Therefore, improving the eco-syetem is an important part of the government's Western Region Development strategy.

1. 锡林郭勒草原
   Xilin Gol Prairie
2. 内蒙坝上
   Bashang Prairie
3. 蒙古包
   Yurts

$$\frac{1 \quad 2}{3}$$

黄土高原

The Loess Plateau

千沟万壑的黄土高原
Bizarre geomorphology on the Loess Plateau

黄土高原位于内蒙古高原以南，北起长城，南达秦岭，东至太行山，西抵祁连山，横跨青海、甘肃、宁夏、陕西、山西、河南等省区，面积约40万平方千米，是中国的第三大高原，平均海拔在800～2 000米。绝大部分的地面覆盖50～80米厚的黄土。在如此大的面积之上，覆盖这么厚的黄土，是大自然创造的一个奇迹。

黄土高原沟壑纵横，崎岖不平。根据地貌的形成过程和特点，可分为陇中高原（也称陇西高原）、陇东陕北高原、山西高原、渭河平原（也称关中平原）。壮观的土柱、奇特的峰丛，以及窑洞和民族风情，都吸引了各地的游客前来参观。

黄土高原的水土流失非常严重，大量的黄土被雨水冲

The Loess Plateau

刷到黄河里，使黄河水中含有大量的泥沙，也使高原表面形成许多沟谷。科学家们的研究结果告诉我们，黄土本身质地疏松，对流水侵蚀的抵抗力极弱，而黄土高原的降水又多为暴雨，侵蚀力非常强。加上不合理的土地利用、滥垦滥伐等人为因素的破坏，更加剧了水土流失。目前，中国政府正通过退耕还林、退耕还草等措施来治理黄土高原上的水土流失。

▶ **你知道吗？** Do you know?

黄土形成于干旱或半干旱的大陆性气候条件下，其物质来源于高原西北部遥远的中亚、蒙古的戈壁和荒漠。干燥、强劲的西北风源源不断地把那些风化形成的细小物质带到东南面来，沿途逐渐堆积下来，年深日久，就形成了黄土高原。

Loess is engendered under the conditions of a dry or semidry continental climate. The substance of the loess comes from faraway Central Asia, the Mongolian Gobi and deserts to the northwest of the plateau. The arid and strong northwest wind keeps bringing the efflorescent particles to the southeast. Those particles are deposited year by year, thus forming the Loess Plateau.

The Loess Plateau is located to the south of the Inner Mongolian Plateau. It borders the Great Wall in the north, the Qinling Mountains in the south, the Taihang Mountains in the east, and the Qilian Mountains in the west, crossing Qinghai, Gansu, Ningxia, Shaanxi, Shanxi, Henan and some other provinces. With an area of about 400 000 km^2 and an average altitude between 800 − 2 000 m, the Loess Plateau is the third largest plateau in China. Most part of the plateau is covered with a layer of loess about 50 − 80 m thick. With so much loess covering such a large area, the plateau is really a natural miracle.

The Loess Plateau has millions of gullies. It can be subdivided into the Longzhong (also called Longxi) Plateau, the Longdong Shaanbei Plateau, the Shanxi Plateau and the Weihe (also called Guangzhong) Plain, according to the formation process and characteristics. The splendid loess pillars, peculiar peaks, cave dwellings and folk customs attract tourists from everywhere.

On the other hand, the plateau has suffered from a serious loss of water and land erosion. Much of the loess is flushed away into the Yellow River by rain, filling the river with mud and sand, and also carving out many gullies on the plateau. Research shows that exposed to precipitation, especially thunderstorms which often occur on the plateau, the porous loess can hardly avoid becoming eroded by the flowing water. This has been exacerbated by man-made devastation such as unreasonable land utilization and excessive deforestation. Now, the Chinese government is taking measures to reforest some of the cultivated land and plant grass to control the loss of water and erosion.

云贵高原

The Yunnan-Guizhou Plateau

云贵高原主要分布在云南、贵州省境内，面积约40万平方千米，平均海拔1 000～2 000米，是中国的第四大高原。

众多的河流穿插在云贵高原上，不停地切割着地面，形成许多又深又陡的峡谷。云贵高原西高东低。云南境内的高原地形相对完整，多为山间小盆地；贵州境内的高原地形支离破碎，崎岖不平，人们常用"地无三里平"来形容这种状况。

盆地内土层深厚而肥沃，是农业比较发达的地方，高原上的城镇也都集中在这里。

云贵高原分布着广泛的喀斯特地貌，它是石灰岩在高温多雨的条件下，经过漫长的岁月，被水溶解和侵蚀而逐渐形成的。地下和地表分布着许多溶洞、暗河、石芽、石笋、峰林等喀斯特地貌。云贵高原是世界上喀斯特地貌发育最完美、最典型的地区之一。

The **Yunnan-Guizhou** Plateau

1. 云贵高原上的梯田
   Terrace on the Yunnan-Guizhou Plateau

2. 地下溶洞
   An underground cave

With an area of about 400 000 km² and an average altitude of 1 000 – 2 000 m, the Yunnan-Guizhou Plateau is located in Yunnan and Guizhou provinces and is the fourth largest plateau in China.

A great number of rivers have scoured out many deep and steep valleys on the Yunnan-Guizhou Plateau as it descends from west to east. The plateau terrain in Yunnan Province is comparatively complete, mostly in the form of small basins among the mountains. The plateau in Guizhou Province, however, is bumpy and irregular, hence goes the saying that, "in Guizhou there is no flat ground over three *li* (meaning half a kilometer, Chinese unit of length)".

The basins have deep and fertile soil where agriculture is well developed and towns are concentrated there.

Karst topography is widely distri-buted on the Yunnan-Guizhou Plateau. Karst forms gradually when limestone is dissolved and eroded by water over a long period of time under high temperature and plentiful rain. There are many caves, underground rivers, stone shoots, stalagmites and other karst topography. The Yunnan-Guizhou Plateau is one of the areas where the karst topography has developed most completely and typically in the world.

东北 平原

The Northeast China Plain

东北平原是中国最大的平原，位于东北地区中部，总面积约35万平方千米。平原东西两侧为长白山地和大兴安岭山地，北部为小兴安岭山地，南端濒临辽东湾。

东北平原处于温带和暖温带范围，有大陆性和季风型气候特征。夏季短促而温暖多雨；冬季漫长而寒冷少雪。冬夏之间季风交替。

东北平原以黑土著称。黑土含有大量的有机质，人们形容它"用手一捏直冒油，插根柴禾也发芽"，这里是中国重要的粮食、大豆、畜牧业生产基地。地下蕴藏石油、煤炭等丰富的矿产资源。这里也是钢铁、机械、能源、化工基地。著名的大庆油田就位于它的北部。

The **Northeast China** Plain

The Northeast China Plain is the biggest plain in China. It is situated in central Northeast China, with an area of about 350 000 km². It is bordered by the Changbai Moutains in the east, Daxing'anling Mountains in the west, Xiaoxing'anling Moutains in the north and the Liaodong gulf in the south.

The Northeast China Plain is in temperate and warm temperate zones, bearing the characteristics of continental climate as well as monsoon climate. The summer there is short, warm, and rainy, and the winter is long, cold with little snow. The monsoons change between summer and winter.

The Northeast China Plain is famous for its black soil, which contains a lot of organic substances. People describe it in such words as "the soil there is so fertile that it oozes oil with just a nip; even a piece of firewood could bud when stuck in the soil". The Northeast China Plain is an important base for grain, soy bean and husbandry in China. It also abounds in oil, coal and other mineral resources under its ground. It is the base for steel and iron, mechanics, energy resources and chemical engineering. The famous Daqing Oilfield is located in the north of the plain.

● 小资料 Data

东北平原可以分为 3 部分：东北部是由黑龙江、松花江和乌苏里江冲积而成的三江平原；北部为松花江和嫩江及其支流冲积而成的松嫩平原；南部为辽河水系冲积而成的辽河平原。

The Northeast China Plain can be divided into three parts. The northeast part is the Sanjiang Plain formed by the Heilongjiang River, Songhuajiang River and Ussouri River's alluvial deposits. The north part is the Songnen Plain formed by the alluviation of the Songhuajiang River and Nenjiang River and their tributaries. The south part is the Liaohe Plain formed by the alluviation of the Liaohe River system.

1 | 2

1. 肥沃的黑土地
   The fertile black soil
2. 广袤的农田
   Vast farmland

华北 平原

The North China Plain

　　华北平原是中国东部大平原的重要组成部分，又叫做黄淮海平原，面积大约 31 万平方千米，是中国的第二大平原。

　　华北平原地势平坦，河湖众多，黄河、淮河、海河为最主要的几条河流。这里交通便利，经济发达，在古代就是中国政治、经济、文化中心，现在中国的首都北京就位于大平原北部，很多重要的城市也在华北平原上。

　　过去，这里许多地方经常发生旱涝灾害，有"大雨大灾，小雨小灾，无雨旱灾"之说。经过中国政府大力发展水利事业，现在这里已经初步建成了一套完整的排水防旱系统，极大地改变了本地区多灾多难的面貌。如今，这里已成为著名的粮食和棉花产地。

The **North China** Plain

The North China Plain is an important part of the big plain in eastern China. Also known as the Huanghuaihai Plain, it has an area of about 310 000 km², being the second largest plain in China.

The North China Plain has a flat terrain. There are many rivers and lakes, among which the Yellow River, Huaihe River and Haihe River are the major ones. Here transportation is convenient and the economy is well developed. The plain has been China's political, economic, and cultural center since ancient times. Now Beijing, China's capital, is in the north of the plain. Many important cities are also located here.

In the past, many places in the North China Plain suffered from floods and drought. As the saying goes, "a big disaster occurs when it rains hard, a small disaster arises when it drizzles, and drought comes when there is no rain". In recent decades, the Chinese government has been developing water conservancy projects and has built up a comprehensive system to deal with floods and droughts. These measures have greatly changed the situation in the past, and now the area has become a famous grain and cotton producing area.

▶ 小知识 Knowledge

华北平原主要是由黄河、淮河、海河三条大河带来的巨量泥沙逐渐向东冲击而成，是典型的冲积平原。

The North China Plain is a typical alluvial plain which is formed by large amount of mud and sand brought down by the Yellow River, Huaihe River and Haihe River.

1. 丰收
   A harvest
2. 华北平原
   The North China Plain

1 | 2

长江 中下游 平原

The Middle and Lower Yangtze Valley Plain

长江中下游平原位于湖北宜昌以东的长江中下游沿岸，面积约20万平方千米，是中国的第三大平原。

长江天然水系及纵横交错的人工河渠使本区成为全国河网密度最大的地区，也是中国淡水湖群分布最集中的地区，著名淡水湖有鄱阳湖、洞庭湖、太湖、洪泽湖及巢湖等。湖沼地区有丰富的水生生物资源，是中国水生植物分布最广、产量最大的地区，淡水水生动物也居全国首位。

长江中下游平原是中国重要的粮、油、棉生产基地，这里水田连片，盛产水稻，加上淡水渔业发达，是中国著名的鱼米之乡。

这里人口众多，城市密集，交通便利，经济繁荣，武汉、长沙、南京、上海等重要城市都分布在这里。

The Middle and Lower
Yangtze Valley Plain

The Middle and Lower Yangtze Valley Plain lies along the middle and lower reaches of the Yangtze River, east of Yichang city, Hubei Province. It has an area of about 200 000 km² and is the third largest plain in China.

The natural system of the Yangtze River, together with crisscrossed man-made rivers and canals, makes this region one of the most densely distributed river networks in China. This is also the area where most of China's freshwater lakes are concentrated. The famous freshwater lakes include the Poyang Lake, Dongting Lake, Taihu Lake, Hongze Lake, Chaohu Lake and so on. The lake and swamp areas abound in aquatic creatures. So this region has the most widely distributed and the largest production of aquatic plants. Its production of freshwater animals also ranks first in the country.

This region is China's major producer of grain, oil and cotton. There are boundless paddy-fields yielding large amounts of paddy. Freshwater fishery is also well developed here. It is a famous land of fish and rice in China.

The Middle and Lower Yangtze Valley Plain has a large population and densely distributed cities. It also has a very convenient transportation system and a prosperous economy. Important cities like Wuhan, Changsha, Nanjing and Shanghai are located here.

1. 江南水乡
   A landscape of Jiangnan (south of the lower reaches of the Yangtze River)
2. 油菜花
   Rape in full flower

1 | 2

塔里木盆地

The Tarim Basin

塔里木盆地位于天山、昆仑山、阿尔金山与帕米尔高原之间，面积约53万平方千米，是中国也是世界上最大的内陆盆地。盆地四周被高山环绕，气候极端干旱。塔里木盆地从边缘到内部形成了典型的环状结构，由外向内依次为砾石戈壁带、绿洲带、沙漠。

盆地的外围是由碎石组成的戈壁滩。戈壁滩的透水性极强，夏季高山冰雪的融水流到这里就渗到了地下，所以戈壁滩的地表总是干涸的。在戈壁滩内侧，绿洲断断续续，组成一条环状的绿洲带。绿洲内水草丰茂，渠道纵横，林木成网，农田成片，经济发达，盆地内的人们主要居住在这里。塔里木盆地里石油、天然气资源蕴藏量十分丰富。

塔克拉玛干沙漠

塔克拉玛干沙漠位于塔里木盆地内部，东西长约1 000千米，南北宽约400千米，面积约33万平方千米，是中国面积最大的沙漠，也是世界居第二位的流动沙漠。在塔克拉玛干沙漠上可以看到各种各样的沙丘，高度一般超过100米，有的可达二三百米。沙漠地区非常干旱，甚至终年无雨，生存条件极为恶劣。

The **Tarim** Basin

● 小资料 Data

讨去认为"塔里木"是维吾尔语"田地"、"种田"的意思。新的研究成果认为,"塔里木"是"流入湖内和沙漠的支流"的意思。

The word"Tarim"used to be considered as "farmlands"or"tilling farmlands"in Uygur. The latest research suggests that"Tarim" means the"tributaries that flow into lakes and deserts".

● 你知道吗? Do you know?

塔里木盆地的地下埋藏着大量的石油,人们称它为"油海"。近年来,来这里考察的科学家和探险家越来越多。

Rich oil deposits are found under the Tarim Basin so that people call the basin an"oil sea". In recent years, more and more scientists and explorers have traveled here for exploration.

The Tarim Basin, encircled by the Tianshan Mountains, the Kunlun Mountains, the Altun Mountains and the Pamirs, and with a total area of about 530 000 km², is the largest inland basin in the world. Because it is surrounded by mountains, the weather here is extremely dry. It has a typical ring structure from its rim to center. From its exterior to the interior, there are gravel gobi, oases and deserts respectively.

The periphery of the basin is gobi land made up of stone fragments. The gobi land can be permeated by water easily. In summer, the melted ice and snow from the high mountains flows down and permeates the ground so that the surface of the gobi is always dry. Within the gobi land, there are intermittent oases forming a ring-like belt. The oases have luxuriant grass and crisscross water channels, and a network of trees and fields. There is a well-developed economy, and people in the basin mainly live here. The Tarim Basin has a rich reserve of petroleum and natural gas.

The Taklamakan Desert

The Taklamakan Desert, located in the Tarim Basin, is about 1 000 km long from east to west and about 400 km wide from south to north. It has an area of about 330 000 km² and is the largest desert in China, and the second largest flowing desert in the world. Various dunes can be found in the Taklamakan Desert. The average height of the dunes is more than 100 m and some can be 200 or 300 m high. It is very dry in the desert areas, and sometimes it doesn't rain for a whole year. Thus the living conditions are extremely adverse.

1. 沙漠地区生存条件恶劣
   The desert
2. 戈壁滩
   The Gobi

1 | 2

准噶尔盆地

The Junggar Basin

准噶尔盆地位于新疆维吾尔自治区北部，天山和阿尔泰山之间，面积约38万平方千米，是中国的第二大盆地。它东高西低，是个半封闭型的盆地。盆地中心是中国的第二大沙漠——古尔班通古特沙漠。

盆地的地下埋藏丰富的石油，早在20世纪50年代就开发了著名的克拉玛依油田。这里还有煤和各种金属矿藏，北部的阿尔泰山区就盛产黄金。

准噶尔盆地
The Junggar Basin

The **Junggar** Basin

The Junggar Basin lies between the Tianshan Mountains and the Altai Mountains in the north of Xinjiang Uygur Autonomous Region. It has an area of about 380 000 km² and is the second largest basin in China. It is a half-closed basin high in the east and low in the west. In the center of this basin is China's second largest desert—the Gurbantünggüt Desert.

In the basin there are rich underground oil deposits. Early in the 1950s, the famous Karamay Oilfield was explored. There are also coal mines and other metal mines here. The Altai Mountains area in the north abounds in gold ores.

柴达木 盆地

The Qaidam Basin

　　柴达木盆地位于青藏高原东北部的青海省境内，面积约 20 万平方千米，是中国第三大盆地。盆地底部平均海拔 2 600 ～ 3 000 米，是中国海拔最高的大盆地。盆地底部平坦开阔，骑马或驾车就像是在平原上行驶一样。

　　这里有丰富的矿产资源，人们称它为"聚宝盆"。盐、石油、铅锌和硼砂是盆地中的"四大宝"。这里的盐特别多，大大小小的盐湖有 100 多个，食盐总储量有 600 亿吨之多。在这里我们可以看到用盐铺设的飞机场和用盐盖的房屋。

The Qaidam Basin

柴达木盆地
The Qaidam Basin

There are rich mineral resources in the Qaidam Basin, so people call it the "treasure bowl". Salt, oil, lead zinc and borax are the four treasures in the basin.

There is so much salt there. There are more than 100 salt lakes and the total salt reserves amount to 60 billion tons. Here we can even see an airport and houses built with salt.

The Qaidam Basin, the third largest basin in China, has an area of about 200 000 km². It is located in Qinghai Province, northeast of the Qinghai-Tibet Plateau. The average altitude of the bottom of the basin is about 2 600 — 3 000 m. It is the highest basin in China. The bottom of the basin is wide and flat so that people feel like crossing an ordinary plain when they drive cars or ride horses in the basin.

▶ 你知道吗？ Do you know?

"柴达木"是蒙古语，意思就是"盐泽"。

"Qaidam"means"salt lake"in the Mongolian language.

四川盆地

The Sichuan Basin

四川盆地是一个群山环绕的完整盆地，平均海拔300～600米，是中国的第四大盆地，也是中国各大盆地中形态最典型、纬度最南、海拔最低的盆地。它位于四川省东部，长江上游，面积20余万平方千米。

盆地内气候冬暖夏热，温差小，雨量充沛，冬季多云雾。西北部有一片长约200千米，宽40～70千米的平原，这就是著名的成都平原。这里有举世闻名的都江堰工程，灌溉着肥沃的土地，自古农业发达，物产丰富，素有"天府之国"的美称。

The **Sichuan** Basin

The Sichuan Basin is an intact basin surrounded by mountains, with an average altitude of about 300 to 600 m. It is the fourth largest basin in China. It has the most typical terrain, the southernmost position, and the lowest altitude among China's big basins. With an area of about 200 000 km², it is located in the east of Sichuan Province, and at the upper reaches of the Yangtze River.

The climate of the basin is warm in winter and hot in summer, with small temperature differences and plenty of rain. In winter, it is mostly cloudy and foggy. There is a 200 km-long and 40 — 70 km-wide plain in the northwest of the basin, which is the famous Chengdu Plain where the world-famous Dujiang Weirs is also built there to irrigate the fertile land. Since ancient times, the Chengdu Plain has had well-developed agriculture and abundant products, enjoying the reputation as "Land of Abundance".

▶ 你知道吗？ Do you know?

四川盆地的内部，丘陵起伏，从山上到山下多是紫红色的砂页岩及其风化后形成的泥土，放眼望去满山遍野都是紫红色的，所以人们称它为"紫色盆地"。

In the Sichuan Basin, the hills are undulating. From the top to the foot of the hills are the purplish red arenaceous shale and the mud formed by the weathering shale. If you take a broad view of the basin, everywhere is purplish red, so people call it the"purple basin".

1. 都江堰
   The Dujiang Weirs
1 | 2
2. 四川盆地概貌
   The Sichuan Basin

长江

The Yangtze River

长江发源于青藏高原唐古拉山主峰——各拉丹冬雪峰，流经青海、西藏、四川、云南、重庆、湖北、湖南、江西、安徽、江苏、上海等 11 个省、市、自治区，最后注入东海，全长 6 300 多千米，是中国第一大河、世界第三长河。

长江上游落差大，水流急，有许多高山耸立的峡谷地段，著名的有虎跳峡、三峡等。出三峡后，进入中游的平原地区。这里江面变宽，水流减缓，多曲流、多支流、多湖泊是这一段的主要特征。长江下游地区地势低平，江阔水深，是著名的鱼米之乡。长江入海口，江面宽达 80 ~ 90 千米，水天一色，极为壮观。中国大部分的淡水湖分布在长江中下游地区。

长江流域水力资源丰富，在葛洲坝和三峡等处都建设了水力发电站。长江具有巨大的航运价值，被称为"黄金水道"，而且两岸的自然风光绚丽多姿，名胜古迹众多。长江流域物产丰富，经济发达。上海、南京、武汉、重庆等大城市都分布在这里。

虎跳峡

虎跳峡位于云南省丽江纳西族自治县境内，长约 16 千米，两岸山岭高出江面 3 000 米以上，水流落差达 200 米。江面最窄处不到 30 米，传说有巨虎一跃而过，所以被称为"虎跳峡"。

The Yangtze River

The Yangtze River originates from snowy Geladandong, the main peak of the Tanggula Mountains on the Qinghai-Tibet Plateau. It runs through 11 provinces, cities and autonomous regions, i.e. Qinghai, Tibet, Sichuan, Yunnan, Chongqing, Hubei, Hunan, Jiangxi, Anhui, Jiangsu and Shanghai, before finally flowing into the East China Sea. With a length of more than 6 300 km, it is the largest river in China and the third longest river in the world.

The upper reaches of the Yangtze River feature big vertical drops, with torrents and many gorges flanked by towering mountains, such as the Tiger-Leaping Gorge, Three Gorges and so on. After the Three Gorges, it gets to the plain area in the middle reaches of the river. Here the river broadens and the flow slows down. This part is characterized with many crooked streams, branches and lakes. Known as fertile land of fish and rice, the lower reaches of the Yangtze River are low and flat, and the water is broad and deep. At the spot where the Yangtze River enters the sea, the river is 80 to 90 km wide, where the water and sky blend into a mixture, presenting a grand view of extraordinary splendor. Most freshwater lakes of China are scattered over the middle and lower reaches of the Yangtze River.

The drainage area of the Yangtze River has an abundance of water power resources. Hydraulic power plants are constructed at the Gezhouba Dam, Three Gorges, etc. Reputed as the Golden Water Route, the Yangtze River has not only a high value for shipping, but also numerous scenic and historical sites. The drainage area of the Yangtze River is rich in products and the economy is well developed. Many metropolises such as Shanghai, Nanjing, Wuhan and Chongqing are distributed along the river.

The Tiger-Leaping Gorge

Located in Lijiang Naxi Autonomous County of Yunnan Province, the Tiger-Leaping Gorge is about 16 km long. The mountains on both banks of the gorge rise over 3 000 m above the river and the drop of the roaring river is up to 200 m. At its narrowest point, the gorge is only 30 m wide. It is said that there was once a huge tiger that got over it in one leap, hence the name "Tiger-Leaping Gorge".

1 | 2

1. 长江
   The Yangtze River
2. 长江源头
   The source of the Yangtze River

黄河

The Yellow River

黄河发源于青海省巴颜喀拉山脉雅拉达泽山麓，流经青海、四川、甘肃、宁夏、内蒙古、山西、陕西、河南、山东等9个省、自治区，注入渤海，全长5 400多千米，是中国的第二长河。从地图上看，黄河的形状是一个巨大的"几"字。

黄河上游有许多峡谷，如龙羊峡、刘家峡、青铜峡等。这些峡谷地带水力资源丰富，建有多座大型水电站。黄河中游经过黄土高原，这里水土流失严重，河水中的泥沙含量大，河水浑浊呈黄色而得名黄河。黄河下游主要流经低缓的华北平原，这里河道宽阔，水流变缓，泥沙大量沉积，形成了河床比两岸高的"地上河"。

黄河流域上游草原辽阔，是中国羊毛、皮革和其他畜产品的主要产地。中、下游是中国农业发源地之一。黄河鲤鱼非常有名，另外还出产毛虾、对虾等20多种水产品。黄河流域还蕴藏有煤、石油和铁等矿藏，中游的山西省被称作"煤海"。

壶口瀑布

壶口瀑布位于山西和陕西的交界处。由于黄河长年的侵蚀和冲击，这里的河底形成了一个直径约50米、深30～50米宽的圆形深潭。当地把这个深潭称为石壶，壶口瀑布即源于此。从北面奔流而来的滔滔黄河，河床由300米宽乍缩为50余米。河水飞流直下，跌入深潭，就像翻腾的黄河水倾倒在一个巨壶之中，所以人们说"天下黄河一壶收"。

▶ **你知道吗？ Do you know?**

黄河是中华民族的母亲河，黄河流域被称为中华民族的摇篮，也是世界文明的发祥地之一。相传中华民族的始祖之一的黄帝就出生在这里。这里还流传着很多关于中华文明起源的故事，传说人就是天神女娲用黄河泥捏成的。

The Yellow River is considered the Mother River of the Chinese people. The drainage area of the Yellow River is honored as the cradle of the Chinese people and also one of the origins of world civilization. It is said that Huangdi (Yellow Emperor, legendary ruler and ancestor of the Chinese nation) was born here. This is the place where numerous legends about the Chinese civilization originated. It was said that man was made by Nv Wa (a legendary goddess in ancient times) with the mud in the Yellow River.

1. 黄河
   The Yellow River
2. 黄河沿岸的农田
   The farmland along the Yellow River

1 | 2

The Yellow River

The Yellow River originates from the foot of the Ya-gradagzê Mountain of the Bayakala Range in Qinghai Province, passing through nine provinces and autonomous regions, i.e Qinghai, Sichuan, Gansu, Ningxia, Inner Mongolia, Shanxi, Shaanxi, Henan and Shandong, and flows into the Bohai Sea. Altogether it is over 5 400 km long and is the second longest river in China. Seen from the map, the Yellow River lies in the shape of huge " 几 (a Chinese character)".

There are many gorges on its upper reaches, such as the Longyangxia Gorge, the Liujiaxia Gorge and the Qingtongxia Gorge. Such areas have abundant water resources, and large-scale hydroelectric power stations have been built there.

The middle reaches flow through the Loess Plateau, where there is a serious problem of soil erosion.

This part of the river contains large amounts of sand. The water here is turbid and shows the yellow color, so the river gets the name "the Yellow River". The Yellow River flows through the North China Plain in its lower reaches, where the river broadens, the flow slows down, and the mud and the sand accumulate to form a "suspending river" where the riverbed is actually higher than the surrounding land.

In the drainage area of the upper reaches of the Yellow River, there are vast grasslands which are the main producing area of wool, leather and other livestock products. The middle and lower reaches are one of the origins of China's agriculture. The river is the native haunt of the Yellow River carp. It also has more than 20 aquatic products such as shrimp and prawns. Apart from those mentioned above, the drainage area of the Yellow River also abounds in mineral resources like coal, oil, iron and so on. Shanxi Province, located in the middle reaches of the Yellow River, is called the "sea of coal".

The Hukou (Kettle Mouth) Waterfalls

The Hukou Waterfalls is located at the juncture of Shanxi and Shaanxi provinces. Due to the erosion and alleviation of the Yellow River, a 30 – 50 m-deep round pool with a diameter of 50 m is formed in the bottom of the river. Local people call the deep pool the "stone kettle" and hence the Hukou Waterfalls. The billowing Yellow River flows from the north to here when the riverbed suddenly constricts from 300 m to 50m. The river descends abruptly and falls into the deep pool. The scene is like pouring down the turbulent Yellow River into a huge kettle. Hence goes the saying that "the boundless Yellow River falls into a small kettle".

1. 壶口瀑布
   Hukou Waterfalls

1 | 2

2. 九曲黄河
   The Yellow River in zigzag course

雅鲁藏布江

The Yarlung Zangbo River

雅鲁藏布江是中国最高的大河之一，发源于喜马拉雅山北麓，在中国境内长 2 057 千米。

雅鲁藏布江的上游是高寒地带。这里河谷开阔，大部分是平浅的谷地，水流缓慢，多湖塘沼泽。这里有原始的大面积草场，是天然的动物乐园，生活着藏羚羊、岩羊、野驴、野牦牛等许多野生动物。

中游地带，河谷宽窄相间，像串珠子一样。

在下游地区，江水绕过喜马拉雅山东段的高山，折向南流，形成了世界上最大的峡谷——雅鲁藏布大峡谷。峡谷形状呈马蹄形，以雄伟、险峻和奇特闻名于世。

The **Yarlung Zangbo** River

The Yarlung Zangbo River is one of the highest rivers in China, originating from the northern peaks of the Himalayas. The part flowing in Chinese territory is 2 057 km long.

The upper reaches of the Yarlung Zangbo River is in a frigid zone. With broad river valleys and flat and shallow water, the current is slow and there are many lakes and swamps. This large area of aboriginal grassland is a paradise for wild animals, such as the Tibetan antelope, blue sheep, wild donkeys and wild yaks.

In the middle reaches of the river, narrow river valleys alternate with broad ones, like a string of beads.

In the lower reaches, the river bypasses high mountains in the eastern part of the Himalayas and turns south, forming the largest canyon in the world—the Yarlung Zangbo Canyon. The canyon is in the shape of a horse's hoof and it is renowned for its majesty, steepness and peculiar charm.

▶ 小资料 Data

雅鲁藏布江流域是藏族文化的发源地，有拉萨、日喀则、江孜和林芝等重要文化和旅游城市。

The drainage area of the Yarlung Zangbo River is the original place of the Tibetan culture. Important cities of culture and tourism, such as Lhasa, Xigazê, Gyangzê and Nyingchi are located here.

1. 雅鲁藏布江
   The Yarlung Zangbo River

2. 雅鲁藏布江上游水流缓慢
   The gently flowing stream in the upper reach of the Yarlung Zangbo River

2
1

京杭运河

The Beijing-Hangzhou Canal

京杭运河
The Beijing–Hangzhou Canal

　　京杭运河北起北京，南到杭州，流经北京、天津、河北、山东、江苏、浙江等6个省、市，沟通了海河、黄河、淮河、长江、钱塘江五大水系，全长1 782千米，是世界上开凿最早、里程最长、工程最大的人工运河。

　　京杭运河对中国南北地区之间的经济、文化发展与交流起到了巨大作用。大运河沿线人口稠密，农业发达。中国近代修建的很多重要铁路和公路都与运河息息相通，各地工业也逐渐兴起。运河流域城镇密集，是精英荟萃的地方。

　　在古代中国，北方人如果到南方去，很多时候就是坐船走水路，其中一段就是在大运河上，沿途风景非常迷人。

The **Beijing-Hangzhou** Canal

The Beijing-Hangzhou Canal extends from Beijing in the north to Hangzhou in the south, covering six provinces and cities of Beijing, Tianjin, Hebei, Shandong, Jiangsu and Zhejiang, and connecting the five great water systems of the Haihe River, the Yellow River, the Huaihe River, the Yangtze River and the Qiantang River. With a total length of 1 782 km, it is the first man-made canal in the world, of the longest mileage and the biggest engineering.

The Beijing-Hangzhou Canal plays an important role in strengthening the communication of economy and culture between China's southern region and northern region. In the areas along the canal are densely populated settlements and well-developed agriculture. Many important railways and highways built in modern times are closely connected by the canal. The industry in the areas around the canal is experiencing an upsurge. Cities and towns are densely distributed around the canal, attracting galaxies of elites to dwell on this area.

In ancient China, taking boat was a good choice for the northerners to travel down to the south. A considerable part of their journey was spent on the Beijing-Hangzhou Canal, with attractive landscapes on the way.

▶ 小资料　Data

古代开凿京杭运河主要是为了将南方的粮食等物资运到北方。1911年津浦铁路开通后，运河的交通价值大大下降。现在，除江苏、浙江境内的河段仍是重要的水上运输线外，其他地段已不能通航。

In ancient times, the Beijing-Hangzhou Canal was dug to ship grain and other materials from the south to the north. After the Tianjin-Huangpu Railway was put into use in 1911, the canal quickly lost its transportation value. Now, except for the part in Jiangsu and Zhejiang where it is still an important transportation route, the rest of the canal is no longer available for navigation.

鄱阳湖

Poyang Lake

　　鄱阳湖位于江西省北部，北通长江，面积 2 933 平方千米，是中国最大的淡水湖。壮阔的鄱阳湖与湖口的石钟山、湖滨的庐山及滔滔奔流的长江一起构成了一幅以大湖、名山、巨川为中心内容的宏伟画卷。

　　鄱阳湖水面广阔，饵料丰富，气候湿润，是白鹤、天鹅、白鹳等多种珍稀鸟类的理想越冬场所。如今，湖畔兴建了候鸟观赏台，"湖畔观鸟"已成为湖区的一大胜景。

Poyang Lake

Poyang Lake, the largest freshwater lake in China, is located in northern Jiangxi Province. With an area of 2 933 km², the lake is connected to the Yangtze River in the north.

The vast Poyang Lake, together with the Stone Bell Mountain at the entrance of the lake, Mount Lushan on its banks and the surging Yangtze River, forms a splendid picture featuring the large lake, the famous mountain and the great river.

The lake is very broad and rich in resources of fish. Due to its humid weather, it is also an ideal place for white cranes, swans, white storks and many other rare birds to spend their winters. A terrace has now been built on the lake side for watching the migratory birds, and it has become one of the most spectacular scenic spots in the area.

▶ 小资料 Data

鄱阳湖古称彭泽、彭湖，后因湖中有鄱阳山而改为鄱阳湖。

Poyang Lake was called Pengze Damp or Penghu Lake in ancient times; later, it was renamed after the Poyang Hill in the middle of the lake.

1. 晚霞中的鄱阳湖
   Poyang Lake in dusk
2. 鄱阳湖渔民晚归
   A fisherman returns from Poyang Lake.

1 | 2

洞庭湖

Dongting Lake

　　洞庭湖位于湖南省北部、长江南岸，面积2 432平方千米。洞庭湖区山川秀美，人杰地灵，名胜古迹较多。著名的岳阳楼就坐落于此，素有"洞庭天下水，岳阳天下楼"之誉。

岳阳楼
The Yueyang Tower

Dongting Lake

Dongting Lake, with an area of 2 432 km², is located in northern Hunan Province to the south of the Yangtze River. Here, there are graceful mountains and rivers, outstanding personages and many famous scenic and historical sites. The famous Yueyang Tower, located at lake side is immortalized in the lines, "the most beautiful lake under heaven is Dongting, the greatest tower under heaven is Yueyang".

▶ 你知道吗？ Do you know?

据唐、宋时期的文献记载，洞庭湖方圆七八百里，故有后来的"八百里洞庭"之说。洞庭湖原是中国第一大淡水湖，但由于泥沙长期淤积等原因，湖而日趋减小。

According to the records in the Tang and Song Dynasties, Dongting Lake was 700 to 800 li (half a kilometer) in circumference. That is why it was called "the 800 li Dongting Lake". Dongting Lake used to be the largest freshwater lake in China, but it shrinks day by day due to the accumulation of silt and other reasons.

太湖

Taihu Lake

太湖位于江苏、浙江两省交界处，面积2 425平方千米。湖区有48岛、72峰，湖光山色，相映生辉，有"太湖天下秀"之称。太湖平原气候温和湿润，土壤肥沃，水网密布，是著名的"鱼米之乡"。太湖周围有苏州、无锡等著名的城市。

Taihu Lake

Lying at the juncture of Jiangsu and Zhejiang provinces, Taihu Lake has an area of 2 425 km². There are 48 islets and 72 peaks in the lake area. The lake and the mountains delightfully set each other off. The lake is reputed to be "the most graceful lake in China". The Taihu Lake Plain has a mild and moist climate, fertile soil and a network of waterways that create a land of fish and rice. Some famous cities such as Suzhou and Wuxi are located at the lakeside.

1. 春到太湖
   Springtime at Taihu Lake

2. 鼋头渚
   Yuantouzhu (Turtle Head Isle)

3. 太湖
   Taihu Lake

1 | 2 | 3

青海湖

Qinghai Lake

　　青海湖，古代称为"西海"，位于青海省东北部，面积 4 340 平方千米，是中国最大的咸水湖，也是中国第一大湖。冬季，湖面封冻，像一面镜子，在阳光下闪闪发光。三月底湖面开始解冻，几场大风过后，湖冰被吹到岸边堆积，好像冰山，是湖区一大奇景。夏秋季节，湖区山青草绿，各种各样的花草将湖滨点缀得非常漂亮。湖中的鸟岛和海心山是候鸟最为集中的地方，多时可达 10 万只。

青海湖鸟岛

　　初夏是到鸟岛观光的最好季节，这时的鸟岛，遍地是各种各样的鸟巢和五光十色的鸟蛋。天上飞的是鸟，地下跑的是鸟，水中游的还是鸟，热闹非凡，非常壮观。

Qinghai Lake

Qinghai Lake, also called the "West Sea" in ancient times, is located in the northeast of Qinghai Province. With an area of 4 340 km², it is the biggest salt lake and also the largest lake in China. In winter, the lake freezes, and it shines like a mirror in the sun. By the end of March, the lake ice begins to melt. Harsh winds can blow the ice to the banks and pile it up in fantastic shapes. In summer and autumn, when the mountains and grass are verdant green, the lake is extremely beautiful decorated by flowers and grasses on the banks. Bird Islet, in the middle of the lake, and Haixin (Heart of the Sea) Mountain attract numerous migratory birds, the numbers of which may be up to 100 000.

Bird Islet in Qinghai Lake

The best time to visit Bird Islet is early summer. At this time, it is covered with various bird nests and colorful bird eggs. Birds are flying in the sky, running on the ground and swimming in the lake, creating a busy and spectacular scene.

▶ 小知识 Knowledge

青海湖，蒙语叫"库库诺尔"，藏语叫"错温波"，都是"青色的海"的意思。青海湖水色青绿，湖滨水草丰美，不少地方已开辟为牧场和农场。

Qinghai Lake is called "koko Nor" in the Mongolian language and "mtsho sngon po" in Tibetan both of which mean "blue green sea". The lake is blue green and has an abundance of aquatic plants along its banks. Many places have been developed into livestock farms and pastures.

1. 青海湖鸟岛
   Bird Islet in Qinghai Lake
2. 青海湖
   Qinghai Lake

1 | 2

台湾岛

Taiwan Island

里盛产稻米，主要经济作物是甘蔗和茶，还有"水果王国"美称，同时产名贵木材。台湾岛四周是海，渔业资源丰富。台湾有丰富的水力、森林、渔业资源。

台湾居民中，汉族占总人口的98%，高山族约占2%。台湾的少数民族统称高山族，分居全省各地。

台湾经济发达，交通便利，美丽富饶，名胜古迹众多，如阿里山、日月潭、乌来瀑布等都是著名的旅游胜地。台湾是中国的"宝岛"。

高山岛

台湾岛上超过3 000米的高山不下百余座，故台湾岛亦被称为"高山岛"。台湾岛有五大山脉，分别是中央山脉、雪山山脉、玉山山脉、阿里山山脉和海岸山脉。

台湾是中国的第一大岛，位于中国东南沿海的大陆架上，东面是太平洋，东北是琉球群岛，南面是巴士海峡，西面有台湾海峡。台湾在西太平洋航道的中心，是中国与太平洋地区各国海上联系的重要交通枢纽。

台湾岛气候冬季温暖，夏季炎热，雨量充沛。北回归线穿过台湾岛中部，北部为亚热带气候，南部属热带气候。这

▶ 小知识 Knowledge

日月潭中有个美丽的小岛，叫光华岛，它把日月潭分为南北两半，北半湖形状像太阳，南半湖像一弯新月，所以叫"日月潭"。

In the Sun-Moon Lake there is a beautiful islet, which is named Splendor Islet. It divides the Sun-Moon Lake into southern and northern parts. The northern part looks like the sun, and the southern one is similar to a crescent; therefore, it is called the Sun-Moon Lake.

阿里山

阿里山主要有森林、云海、日出三大奇观。

故宫博物院

台北市的"故宫博物院"是亚洲古代文物中心之一，院内藏有许多中国古代艺术珍品。

日月潭

日月潭位于台湾中部玉山以北，是台湾第一天然大湖。

湖畔有许多亭台楼阁。潭西的涵碧楼是观赏湖光山色的好地方，潭南的玄奘寺是台湾的佛教胜地。

野柳

台湾岛东北海岸野柳的岩石形状非常奇特，有"女王头"、"仙女鞋"和"乳房石"等48景，令游客惊叹不已，被称为"出自上帝之手的杰作"。五颜六色的贝壳和海胆以及美人蕉、龙舌兰等海岸植物使这里成为一个天然的海岸公园。

1	2
	3

1. 台北
   Taipei
2. 新竹的街道
   A street in Xinzhu, Taiwan
3. 阿里山
   Ali Mountain

Taiwan Island

Taiwan Island is the largest island in China. It is situated on the continental shelf along the southeast coast of China. It is bordered on the east by the Pacific Ocean , on the northeast by the Ryukyu Islands, on the south by the Bashi Channel, and on the west by the Taiwan Strait. At the center of the west Pacific's sea-route, Taiwan serves as the hub connecting China and other countries in the Pacific region.

Taiwan is warm in winter, and hot and rainy in summer. The Tropic of Cancer traverses the island in the middle. North of the line is the subtropical zone, while south of it belongs to the tropical zone. The island is rich in rice, and its main industrial crops are sugar cane and tea. It is reputed to be the "kingdom of fruits". It also produces famous and precious wood. Since Taiwan Island is encircled by seas, it has rich fishing resources. It also has abundant resources of waterpower, forestry and fisheries.

Of the Taiwan inhabitants, the Han nationality makes up 98%, and the ethnic Gaoshan (high mountains) nationality accounts for about 2 % of the total. All the ethnic minorities in Taiwan are called Gaoshan nationality. They are distributed all over the Taiwan province.

Taiwan has a developed economy and convenient transportation. It is a beautiful and richly endowed island. There are many scenic spots and historic sites, such as the Ali Mountain, Sun-Moon Lake, Wulai Waterfalls and so on. Taiwan is indeed China's "treasure island".

Gaoshan Island

There are over 100 high mountains that are more than 3 000 m high on Taiwan Island, so it is also called the Island of High Mountains. There are five big mountain ranges, namely the Central Mountain Range, the Snow Mountain Range, the Jade Mountain Range, the Ali Mountain Range and the Coast Mountain Range.

Ali Mountain

Ali Mountain boasts three marvelous spectacles—the forests, the sea of cloud and the sunrise.

The Palace Museum in Taipei

The Palace Museum in the city of Taipei is one of the ancient cultural relic centers of Asia. It houses numerous rare art treasures from ancient China.

The Sun-Moon Lake

The Sun-Moon Lake is located to the north of the Jade Mountains in the central Taiwan, and it is the largest natural lake in Taiwan.

There are many pavilions, towers and verandas around the lake. The Hanbi (encompassing green jade) Tower, west of the lake, is a place offering a good view of the shimmering lake and charming mountains. The Xuanzang (a famous monk in the Tang Dynasty) Temple, south of the lake, is a Buddhist shrine in Taiwan.

Yeliu Scenic Area

In the Yeliu Scenic Area, on the northeast coast of Taiwan Island, visitors can check out strange rock formations like the famous 48 scenic spots—"Queens Head", "Fairies shoes", "Breast Stone" and so on. Visitors may marvel at these "masterpieces created by God's hands". Colorful shells, sea urchins, and coastal plants like cannas and century plants make this area a natural coastal park.

▶ 小资料 Data

台湾自古以来就是中国不可分割的一部分，三国时期被称为夷洲，明朝才叫台湾。台湾历史上曾多次受到外来侵略，1662 年郑成功收复了台湾。

台湾有"八景十二胜"。八景是玉山积雪、阿里云海、双潭秋月、大屯春色、安平夕照、清水断崖、鲁阁幽峡和澎湖渔火。

Taiwan has been an inseparable part of China since ancient times. In the Three Kingdoms Period (220-280 AD) it was called Yizhou. Not until the Ming Dynasty (1368-1644 AD) was it named Taiwan. It has been invaded many times. In 1662, Zheng Chenggong (1624-1662 AD) recovered Taiwan.

Taiwan has eight scenic spots and 12 attractions. The eight scenic spots are Accumulated Snow on the Jade Mountain, Sea of Cloud in Ali, Autumn Moon of Double Ponds, Spring Scenery in Datun, Sunset in Anping, Precipice in Qingshui, Secluded Canyon of Luge and Fishing Boat Lights in Penghu.

1 | 2

1. 台北 "故宫博物院"
   "The Palace Museum" in Taipei
2. 日月潭
   The Sun-Moon Lake

海南岛

Hainan Island

海南岛在中国的南部，面积3.4万多平方千米。它北隔琼州海峡同雷州半岛相望，是中国第二大岛。海南岛的地形中间高，四周低。五指山是岛上最著名的山脉，从东南方望去，其主峰形似五指，因此而得名。

海南岛到处是一派热带风光。这里有大片的热带森林，植物种类繁多，终年常绿。另外还有许多独特的生物现象，如板状根、老茎生花等。

海南岛是橡胶、椰子、油棕、剑麻、胡椒等热带经济作物的主要产地。

海南岛是著名的旅游胜地，被称为南海上的一颗"明珠"。特别是南部的三亚市，碧水蓝天，景色迷人。亚龙湾、大东海、天涯海角、鹿回头等著名景点，每天都吸引着众多的国内外游人。

海南岛上生活着黎族、苗族、回族、瑶族、壮族等少数民族，其中黎族最多。

Hainan Island

▶ 你知道吗？ Do you know?

海南岛的资源很丰富，这里有中国最著名的富铁矿和莺歌海盐场。从珠江口到北部湾一带的海盆中，还蕴藏着丰富的天然气资源。

Hainan Island has abundant resources, including the most famous high grade iron-mine in China, the Yinggehai Salt Field and the rich natural gas fields that lie under the sea basin from the mouth of the Pearl River to Beibu Gulf.

1 | 2

1. 三亚海滩
   The beach in Sanya
2. 海南的椰风海韵
   Natural scenery of Hainan Island

Hainan Island, the second largest island in China, lies in the far south of China, with an area of over 34 000 km². It faces the Leizhou Peninsula across the Qiongzhou Strait to the north. Hainan Island is high in the middle and low on the rim. The Five-Finger Mountain is the most famous mountain on the island. Seen from the southeast, the mountain's main peak is like five fingers. That is how the mountain gets its name.

You may enjoy tropical scenery everywhere on Hainan. There is a large area of tropical forest, a variety of evergreen plants, plus many special biological phenomena, such as plate-like roots, blossoms on old stems and so on.

Hainan is the main production area for tropical cash crops such as rubber, coconuts, oil palms, sisal and pepper, etc.

It is a famous tourist attraction, reputed as a pearl in the South China Sea. Moreover, Sanya City in the south has green sea water, blue sky and charming scenery. Many famous scenic spots such as Yalong Bay, Great East Sea, Tianyahaijiao (Remote Corner of the Earth) and Luhuitou (Deer's Turning Round), attract thousands of visitors every day.

On the island live the Li, Miao, Hui, Yao and Zhuang peoples. Among these ethnic minorities, the Li has the largest population.

▶ 小资料 Data

海南岛原来是和大陆连在一起的，后因琼州海峡沉陷，才与大陆分离。琼州海峡最窄处只有18千米。

Hainan Island was originally connected to the mainland. Later the land sank to let in the sea and formed the Qiongzhou Strait, whose narrowest part is only 18 km wide.

南海诸岛

The South China Sea Islands

在中国的南海海面上，散布着众多的岛、礁、暗沙，总称为南海诸岛。除个别火山岛外，南海诸岛都由珊瑚礁岛组成，总面积约12平方千米。南海诸岛包括东沙群岛、西沙群岛、中沙群岛、南沙群岛和黄岩岛。

南海诸岛处于太平洋和印度洋、亚洲和大洋洲海上航运的要冲位置，在交通和国防上都有重要的意义。很早以前，中华民族的祖先就在南海诸岛上开始活动并修筑了相应的建筑，中国对南海诸岛拥有主权。

东沙群岛

东沙群岛由东沙岛及南卫滩、北卫滩组成。附近海域水产丰富，有海参、海胆、海星、蚌蛤和海人参草等。中国很早就在岛上建立了观象台和灯塔。

西沙群岛

西沙群岛是南海诸岛中岛屿最多的群岛。岛上生长着多种热带植物，如棕榈、椰子、木瓜、香蕉等。附近海域出产海龟、海参、金枪鱼等水产品，每到鱼汛期，广东、海南一带的渔船便云集于此进行捕捞。

中沙群岛

中沙群岛是一群尚未露出海面的珊瑚礁滩，距海平面约有一二十米。由于珊瑚礁映衬的结果，这一带的海水呈现微绿的颜色。

南沙群岛

南沙群岛由分布很广、数量很多的岛、礁、暗沙组成，主要有太平岛等。岛上生长着

▶ **小资料** Data

南海诸岛附近海域蕴藏着丰富的石油资源。较大的岛上都有很厚的鸟粪层，是鲣鸟的粪便堆积而成的，含磷量很高，是很好的肥料。

The waters near the South China Sea Islands contain abundant oil reserves. The larger islands are covered by thick layers of bird dung, mainly from the brown booby. The dung has high phosphor content and is a good fertilizer.

西沙风光
The scenery of the West Sand Islands

The South China Sea Islands

椰子、木瓜等多种热带植物，附近海域也是南海重要的渔场之一。南端的曾母暗沙位于北纬 4 度附近，是中国领土最南边的地方。

The South China Sea is littered with many islands, reefs and submerged shoals to which the general name South China Sea Islands is given. Except for a few volcanic islands, the South China Sea Islands are made up of coral reef. With the area of about 12 km², the islands include the East Sand Islands, the West Sand Islands, the Middle Sand Islands, the South Sand Islands and the Yellow Rock Island.

The South China Sea Islands stand at the crossroads of the shipping routes between the Pacific and Indian oceans, Asia and Oceania, and are of great importance to transportation and national defense. Long before their settlement, the ancestors of the Chinese people had begun to live there and erect buildings. China has full sovereignty over the South China Sea Islands.

The East Sand Islands

The East Sand Islands comprise the East Sand Island, the Nanwei Shoal and the Beiwei Shoal. The surrounding waters are rich in aquatic products, such

西沙夕照
The West Sand Islands in the dusk

as sea cucumbers, sea urchins, starfish, mussels, clams and sea ginseng weeds, etc. China built observatories and beacons on the islands long ago.

The West Sand Islands

The West Sand Islands form the largest group in the South China Sea Islands, with the largest number of islands. Various tropical plants, such as palms, coconuts, pawpaws and bananas grow there, while the local waters produce turtles, sea cucumbers, tuna and other aquatic products. Every fishing season, boats from Guangdong and Hainan provinces swarm in to fish.

The Middle Sand Islands

The Middle Sand Islands are a group of coral reef shoals lying 10 to 20 m below the sea surface. Against the background of the coral reefs, the seawater here looks slightly green.

The South Sand Islands

The South Sand Islands are a widely distributed, large group of islands, reefs and submerged shoals. The major island is called Taiping Island. On the islands grow coconuts, pawpaws and many other tropical plants, while the surrounding waters are an important fishing site. The Zengmu Reef, located close to the 4th parallel of the northern latitude, is the southernmost point of Chinese territory.

中国七大古都

Seven Ancient Capitals of China

北京

Beijing

北京是中华人民共和国的首都，是全国的政治、文化和科技教育的中心，也是全国的交通和国际交往中心。

北京是世界历史文化名城和古都之一。自938年以来，辽以北京为陪都。此后北京又先后成为金中都、元大都、明清国都。民国初为都城，1928年国民党政府迁都南京，始将北京改为北平市。1949年中华人民共和国成立，恢复北京的名称，并正式定为首都。

中华人民共和国成立50多年来，首都北京的建设日新月异，发生了巨大的变化。现代化建筑如雨后春笋般相继崛起。北京已经成功地获得2008年奥运会的举办权。"绿色奥运、科技奥运、人文奥运"的宗旨，必将给北京带来更大的变化，进一步推动中

国体育运动和世界奥林匹克运动的发展，进一步加强中国人民和世界人民的友好交流。

北京科技力量强大，有中国科学院、北京大学、清华大学等世界著名科研机构和高等学府。同时，北京正大力发展高新技术产业，人才密集的中关村被称为中国的"硅谷"。

长城

长城以它浩大的工程，雄伟的气魄和悠久的历史著称于世，被列为世界奇迹，1987年被联合国教科文组织列入世界文化遗产名录。

故宫

故宫又称紫禁城，是明、清两朝的皇宫，1987年被联合国教科文组织列入世界文化遗产名录。

故宫是世界上最大的皇家宫殿群，内有宫室9 000多间。故宫是中国最大的国家博物馆，也是最丰富的文化和艺术宝库。

宫内藏有大量的历史文物和历代艺术珍品。它的独特建筑风格是中国古代建筑的精华。

颐和园

颐和园是中国著名的古代园林，现已被联合国教科文组织列入世界文化遗产名录。颐和园内有山有水，整体构思巧妙，是世界上罕见的园林杰作。

天坛

天坛于1420年建成，是明、清两代皇帝每年祭天和祈祷五谷丰收的地方。天坛建筑结构奇特，装饰精美，在世界上享有极高的声誉，现已被联合国教科文组织列入世界文化遗产名录。

2

1

1. 天安门
   Tian'anmen
2. 故宫博物院
   The Palace Museum

Beijing

Beijing is the capital of the People's Republic of China. It is the political, cultural, scientific and educational center of the state and also the center of transportation and international exchange.

Beijing is a world-renowned city of history and culture. The Liao Dynasty made Beijing its alternate capital since 938 AD. Later, Beijing became the capital of the Jin Dynasty, called Shangdu, capital of the Yuan Dynasty, known as Dadu, and capital of the Ming and Qing Dynasties. During early Republican period in 1910s it became the capital of the Republic of China. In 1928, the capital was moved to Nanjing and Beijing was renamed Beiping, a name that it held until 1949. After the founding of the People's Republic of China in 1949, Beijing was once again renamed Beijing, and was designated the country's capital.

In the 50-odd years after the founding of the People's Republic of China, the capital has developed quickly and taken on a new look. Modern buildings rise up one by one like bamboo shoots in the spring

after rain. With the successful bid for the Summer Olympic Games in 2008, the concept of "Green Olympics, Technology Olympics and Cultural Olympics" will definitely bring large changes to Beijing, promote the develop-

ment of China's athletic sports and the world's Olympic games, and strengthen the friendly communication between Chinese people and other people in the world.

Beijing possesses a strong force in science and technology. The Chinese Academy of Sciences, Peking University and Tsinghua University are among the world famous scientific research organizations and institutions of higher education. At the same time, Beijing is making efforts to develop its hi-tech industries. The Zhongguancun area, now called China's Silicon Valley, has gathered a galaxy of talents.

The Great Wall

The Great Wall is known for its incomparable grandeur and long history. It is regarded as one of the world wonders. In 1987, it was inscribed on the world cultural heritage list by UNESCO.

The Palace Museum in Beijing

The Palace Museum, also called the Forbidden City, was the royal palace of the Ming and Qing dynasties. In 1987, it was imscribed on the world cultural heritage list by UNESCO.

The Palace Museum is the world's largest royal palace complex, with more than 9 000 rooms inside. The Palace Museum is the biggest national museum in China with the richest cultural and artistic treasures. In it are kept myriads of historical, cultural relics and artistic treasures

of every dynasty. Its unique architectural style is the epitome of Chinese classical architecture.

The Summer Palace (The Garden of Harmonious Nature)

The Summer Palace is a renowned classical garden in China and has been listed as a world cultural heritage site by UNESCO. There are mountains and lakes in the Summer Palace. The ingenious layout makes it a rare masterpiece among the best gardens of the world.

The Temple of Heaven

The Temple of Heaven, built in 1420, was an altar where emperors of the Ming and Qing Dynasties offered sacrifices to heaven and prayed for a good harvest. Enjoying high reputation in the world for its special architecture and delicate decorations, it is listed by UNESCO as a world cultural heritage site.

1	
2	3

1. 人民英雄纪念碑
   The Monument to the People's Heroes
2. 乾清宫的皇帝宝座
   The imperial throne in the Hall of Celestial Purity
3. 日新月异的北京城
   A new look of the modern Beijing

西安

Xi'an

　　西安是陕西省的省会，是我国新兴的工业基地和科教中心城市，也是中国东西交通的枢纽和西北地区重要的城市。

　　西安在八百里秦川中部，南依秦岭，北临渭河，其地势东南高，西北低，市区有多条河流，自古就有"八水绕长安"之美称。

　　西安是我国黄河流域古代文明的重要发源地之一，与雅典、罗马、开罗并称为世界四大古都。西安古称长安，距今已有 3 000 多年的历史。自西周时起直到唐代，先后有 12 个王朝在这里建都，历经 2 000 余年。汉、唐两代，更是西安的鼎盛时期，汉代的长安城相当于古罗马城的 3 倍，唐代的长安城则为汉长安城的 2.4 倍，面积达 84.1 平方千米，人口达百万以上，

是当时世界上规模最大最繁华的城市。中华人民共和国成立后，西安一直是西北的政治中心和陕西省省会所在地。

悠久的历史、发达的文化为西安留下了许多闻名中外的古迹名胜。秦始皇兵马俑地下军阵被誉为"世界第八大奇迹"。还有半坡母系氏族村落遗址、秦始皇陵、乾陵等陵墓以及慈恩寺塔、碑林、华清池等古迹。

西安的工业比较发达，以机械、电子、电器、纺织和国防工业著称全国。同时作为国家历史文化名城，也是旅游热点城市之一。

大雁塔

大雁塔初建为5层，唐代武则天当皇帝时，扩建为10层，后被战火破坏。现存7层，塔高64米，是全国重点保护文物。

华清池

华清池是一个古老而著名的温泉，泉水温度为43℃，含有多种化学成分，对人体有医疗保健作用。

半坡遗址

半坡遗址是黄河流域规模最大、保存最完整的原始社会母系氏族村落遗址。

1. 钟楼
   The Clock Tower
2. 半坡遗址
   The Banpo Ruins

Xi'an

X i'an, the capital of Shaanxi Province, is a new industrial base and scientific and educational center in China. It is the hub of communications between eastern and western China and is an important city in Northwest China.

Xi'an is located in the middle of the 800-li (half a kilometer in Chinese) Qinchuan (old name for what are now Shaanxi and Gansu provinces). It is bordered on the south by the Qinling Mountains, and on the north by the Weihe River, with a terrain sloping from the southeast to the northwest.There are many rivers in the city. Since ancient times, it is celebrated for "eight rivers flowing around Chang'an (the old name for Xi'an in ancient times)".

Xi'an is an important center for the origin of ancient civilization in the drainage area of the Yellow River. Xi'an, together with Athens, Rome and Cairo, are called the world's four great ancient capitals. It was called Chang'an in the ancient time. It has over 3 000 years of recorded history. From the Western Zhou Dynasty to the Tang Dynasty, Xi'an has been the capital of 12 dynasties for 2 000 years. The Han and the Tang Dynasties are considered the zenith of Xi'an.

Chang'an in the Han Dynasty was 2 times larger than ancient Rome. Chang'an in the Tang Dynasty was the largest and most cosmopolitan city in the world, measuring 84.1 km^2, 2.4 times the size of the Han Chang'an, with over one million residents. After the foundation of the People's Republic of China, Xi'an has always been the political center of Northwest China and the capital of Shaanxi Province.

Long history and advanced

culture have endowed the city with numerous world-famous places of historical interest and scenic beauty. The Qinshihuang Terracotta Warriors and Horses are the most famous one, enjoying the title of "the eighth wonder in the world". The other famous

places include the Banpo Museum of Neolithic Relics, Emperor Qin Shihuang's Mausoleum, the Qian Ling Mausoleum, and other historical sites such as the Temple of Great Maternal Grace, the Xi'an Forest of Steles, and the Pool of Glorious Purity.

1 | 2
   | 3

1. 华清池
   The Pool of Glorious Purity
2. 小雁塔
   The Small Wild Goose Pagoda
3. 大雁塔
   The Big Wild Goose Pagoda

Xi'an has a relatively advanced industry. Its machinery, electronics, electrical appliances, textiles and national defense industries are celebrated throughout the country. As a famous city of history and culture, it is also one of the main tourist attractions.

The Big Wild Goose Pagoda

The original Big Wild Goose Pagoda had five storeys. When Wu Zetian (the only empress in Chinese history) came to the throne, it was expanded to 10 storeys. Subsequently, it was devastated by wars and fires. Now it has only seven storeys, with a height of 64 m. It is one of the key cultural relics under the State protection.

The Pool of Glorious Purity

The Pool of Glorious Purity is an old famous hot spring whose temperature is about 43°C. The water in the pool contains various chemical elements that are good for medical treatment and health care.

The Banpo Ruins

The Banpo Ruins is the largest and most complete matrilineal commune of the primitive society that lived in the drainage area of the Yellow River.

洛阳

Luoyang

洛阳位于河南省西部，地处中原，有"天下之中"、"九州腹地"之称。洛阳是华夏文明的重要发祥地之一，因地处洛河之北而得名。

洛阳历史悠久，是国务院首批公布的历史文化名城和中国七大古都之一。洛阳从中国第一个王朝夏朝起，先后有13个王朝在此建都，是中国建都最早、历时最长的古都。隋唐时期，洛阳人口百万，是当时世界上最繁华的大都市之一。

洛阳的名胜古迹很多。沿洛河排列的夏、商、周、汉

魏、隋唐五人都城遗址举世罕见，被誉为"五都荟洛"。另外还有龙门石窟、白马寺、古墓博物馆、王城牡丹园、王城广场、天子驾六博物馆等著名景点。

今大的洛阳也是新兴的工业城市，以拖拉机、矿山机械、轴承工业著称，钢加工、棉纺织、炼油等工业也很发达。同时是陇海、焦柳等铁路的交通枢纽。

龙门石窟

龙门石窟与甘肃的敦煌石窟、山西大同的云冈石窟并称中国古代佛教石窟艺术的三大宝库。龙门石窟凿于北魏孝文帝迁都洛阳（494年）之时，现存佛像十万余尊，窟龛2 300多个。1961年被国务院列为国家重点文物保护单位。

白马寺

白马寺是佛教传入中国后由官方营造的第一座寺院，被誉为中国佛教的"释源"和"祖庭"。

Luoyang

Luoyang lies in the west of Henan province. Situated in the central plain, it is known as "the Gravity Center of China" and "the Hinterland of Nine Divisions (a poetic name for China)". Named due to its location on the north side of the Luohe River, Luoyang is one of the most important places of origin of the Huaxia (archaic name for China) civilization.

With a very long history, Luoyang is among the first Chinese cities with long history and splendid culture listed by the State Council. Luoyang is also one of the seven major ancient capitals in Chinese history. Starting from the Xia Dynasty, the first imperial dynasty in China, it served as the capital for thirteen dynasties. Luoyang was the earliest capital city with the longest time of being capital in China's history. During the Sui and Tang Dynasties, with a population of more than one million, Luoyang was at that time the most prosperous city in the world.

There are a large number of cultural relics and historical sites in Luoyang. Arrayed along the the Luohe River, the capital relics of the Xia, the Shang, the Zhou, the Han and Wei, the Sui and Tang Dynasties present a rare scene in the world, known as "the Five Capitals Assembling in Luoyang City". Moreover, there are the Longmen Grottoes, the Baima (White Horse) Temple, the Museum of Ancient Tombs, the Park of Peonies of the Royal City, etc.

Nowadays Luoyang is a new industrial base in China, famous for its tractors, mineral machines and bearing industry. Besides, it is also well developed in such fields as steel processing, textiles and refining petroleum. Luoyang is also a transportation center of

Longhai railway (Lianyungang-Lanzhou), Jiaoliu railway (Jiaozuo-Liuzhou) and other railways.

The Longmen Grottoes

The Longmen Grottoes, together with the Dunhuang Grottoes in Gangsu Province and the Yungang Grottoes at Datong in Shanxi Province, are known as the three major treasure-houses of Buddhist grotto art in ancient China. In 494 AD, Emperor Xiaowen of the Northern Wei Dynasty moved his capital to Luoyang and started the construction of the Longmen Grottoes. The Grottoes boast a huge collection of more than 100 000 Buddhist statues and 2 300 niches. They were listed as one of the national key cultural relics by the State Council in 1961.

The Baima (White Horse) Temple

The Baima (White Horse) Temple was the first officially built Buddhist shrine since Buddhism was introduced into China. It is reputed as "the Origin of Buddhism" in China.

1 | 2

1. 河南洛阳出土文物
   The cultural relic excavated in Luoyang
2. 龙门石窟
   The Longmen Grottoes

南京

Nanjing

南京是江苏省的省会，也是中国七大古都之一。它风景优美，名胜古迹众多，是中国历史文化名城。

南京历史悠久，东吴、东晋和南朝的宋、齐、梁、陈（史称六朝）以及南唐、明、太平天国、中华民国共 10 个朝代和政权在南京建都。新中国成立后南京为江苏省省会，成为江苏省最大的综合性工业城市。

南京目睹过三国鼎立和六朝兴亡，见证过近代中国的屈辱，也经历了辛亥革命和抗日战争。新中国成立后，南京发展迅速，是长江下游、华东沿海地区对外开放的大工业城市之一，也是著名的水陆交通枢纽。

南京是我国重要的旅游城市，名胜古迹众多，有玄武湖、秦淮河、中山陵、雨花台等。

中华门

中华门是南京城墙的最大城门，由三道瓮城和四道城门组成，南北长 128 米，东西宽 118.5 米，总面积达 15 168 平方米。城墙高 21.45 米，工程宏伟，结构复杂，设计巧妙，在中国城墙建筑史上占有极其重要的地位。

中山陵

中山陵是中国伟大的民主革命先行者孙中山先生的陵墓。陵墓像一个大钟，由南往北沿山势逐渐升高，共有 392 级台阶。整个建筑群布局严整，庄严雄伟，被誉为"中国近代建筑史上的第一陵"。

秦淮河

秦淮河是著名的游览胜地，分为内河和外河。内河在南京城内，是十里秦淮最繁华的地方。秦淮风光最著名的是自明代沿袭至今的灯船。河上的船，不论大小，一律悬挂彩灯。到秦淮河游玩的人，都以乘灯船为乐事。

夫子庙

夫子庙位于秦淮河北岸，始建于 1034 年，原是供奉和祭祀孔子的地方，现已成为群众文化活动场所。夫子庙古建筑群，包括周围的茶馆、酒楼、店铺等建筑都是明清风格。这里的传统食品和风味小吃非常多，品种不下 200 种。

南京长江大桥

南京长江大桥是中国第一座自己设计建造的双层双线公路、铁路两用大桥。整座大桥像一条彩虹凌空江上，十分壮观。它是中国造桥史上的一座里程碑，是中国人民的骄傲。

1 | 2

1. 秦淮河
The Qinhuai River
2. 夫子庙夜景
Confucius Temple at night

Nanjing

Nanjing is the capital of Jiangsu Province, and is also one of the seven ancient capitals in China. It has beautiful scenery and many famous scenic and historic sites.

Nanjing has a long history. The Six dynasties of the Wu, the Eastern Jin, the Song, the Qi, the Liang and the Chen, chose Nanjing as their capital. Later on, the Southern Tang Dynasty, the Ming Dynasty, the Taiping Heavenly Kingdom (1851 — 1864 AD) and the Republic of China also made Nanjing their capital. After the founding of the People's Republic of China, Nanjing became the capital of Jiangsu Province and the largest comprehensive industrial city of this province.

Nanjing witnessed the triangular balance of power of the Three Kingdoms (220 — 280 AD), the ups and downs of six dynasties, the insult inflicted on contemporary China, as well as the Xinhai Revolution of 1911 and the War of Resistance against Japan (1937 — 1945). After the founding of the People's Republic of China, Nanjing has experienced rapid economic growth. It is one of the biggest open industrial cities in the lower reaches of the Yangtze River and the coastal areas of East China. It is also a famous water-land transportation hub.

Nanjing is an important tourist resort in China. Many scenic

and historical sites, such as the Xuanwu Lake, the Qinhuai River, the Sun Yat-sen Mausoleum, and the Terrace of Raining Flowers, are strewn all over this pleasant city.

The Zhonghua Gate

The Zhonghua Gate is the biggest city gate in Nanjing, which is made up of three urn-like city walls and four gates. It is 128 m long from south to north and 118.5 m wide from east to west, covering an area of 15 168 m². The wall, 21.45 m high, is a magnificent project of complicated structure and fine design. It takes a significant position in China's history of city wall construction.

The Sun Yat-sen Mausoleum

Sun Yat-sen Mausoleum is built to commemorate Dr. Sun Yat-sen, the great pioneer of the democratic revolution in China. This mausoleum, like a big bell, ascends from the south to the north by 392 steps. The whole building complex is designed to display a solemn and majestic air, known as "the best mausoleum in the history of Chinese contemporary architecture".

The Qinhuai River

The Qinhuai River, a famous scenic spot, consists of the inner river and outer river. The inner river is in the city of Nanjing, which is the busiest place along the ten-li Qinhuai. The biggest attraction of Qinhuai River is the lantern boats which can be traced back to the Ming Dynasty. All the boats on the river, big or small, hang colorful lanterns up

and everyone visiting here enjoys the pleasure of taking a ride on the boats.

The Confucius Temple

Located on the northern bank of the Qinhuai River, the Confucius Temple was first built in 1034, and was originally a place for enshrining and offering sacrifice for Confucius. Now it has become a place where local people can have some cultural activities. The construction of this ancient complex, including the surrounding teahouses, restaurants and stores, were all built in the style of the Ming and Qing Dynasties. More than 200 different traditional foods and local delicacies are available there.

Nanjing Yangtze River Bridge

Nanjing Yangtze River Bridge is the first double-decker and double-line bridge of road and railway designed and built independently by Chinese people. The whole bridge looks splendid, like a rainbow hanging over the river. It is a milestone in China's history of bridge construction and a pride of Chinese people.

▶ 你知道吗? Do you know?

二三百万年前，雨花台是一个低洼地。河水从上游冲来大量玛瑙卵石，后来地壳抬升，河滩变成高地，美丽的卵石便留在雨花台上了。

Two to three million years ago, the Terrace of Raining Flowers was only a slight depression. A large number of agate pebbles were brought down by water from the upper reaches of a river. Later the earth's crust began to rise, and the river shoals became highland. Since then beautiful pebbles were left on the Terrace of Raining Flowers.

| 1 | 2 |

1. 南京长江大桥
   Nanjing Yangtze River Bridge
2. 中华门
   The Zhonghua Gate

开封

Kaifeng

开封市位于河南省东部，是重要的工商业和文教中心，以化工、机械、轻纺工业著称。

开封市古称汴梁，是中国七大古都之一。据研究，远在新石器时代早期开封一带就有人类活动。后梁、后晋、后汉、后周都曾建都开封。960 年，北宋建立后也定都开封，号称东都。北宋时开封人口达 150 万，不仅是国内经济、政治、文化中心，而且是"万国咸通"的国际大都市。

在漫长的历史长河中，开封素以物华天宝、人杰地灵而著称，其政治、经济、文化的发展，不但对中原地区而且对全国曾产生过巨大的影响。开封历史悠久，名人众多，有蔡邕、蔡文姬、崔颢等。灿烂悠久的历史留给开封丰富的旅游资源，这里的仿古建筑群风格鲜明多样，还有大相国寺、包公祠、朱仙镇岳飞庙等名胜古迹。

包公祠

为纪念执法如山的清官包拯，开封市政府在包公湖畔修建了占地 1 万平方米左右的包公祠，以供后人瞻仰。整个建筑风格古朴，庄严肃穆。

大相国寺

大相国寺是中国著名的佛教寺院，位于开封市中心。北宋时期，大相国寺是京城最大的寺院和全国佛教活动中心。

1. 开封街景
   A street scene in Kaifeng city
2. 大相国寺
   The Daxiangguo Temple

Kaifeng

Kaifeng City is located in Eastern Henan province. It is both a pivotal industrial and commercial center and a cultural and educational center. Kaifeng is celebrated for chemistry, machinery and textile industry.

Formerly named Bianliang, Kaifeng is one of the major seven ancient capitals in China. According to some research, there were human activities around Kaifeng area as early as the New Stone Age. It served as the capital of a number of dynasties such as the Later Liang Dynasty, the Later Jin Dynasty, the Later Han Dynasty and the Later Zhou Dynasty. In 960 AD, the Northern Song Dynasty was founded and made Kaifeng its capital, then known as "Dongdu (Eastern Capital)". During the Northern Song Dynasty, with a population of 1.5 million, Kaifeng was not only the economic, political and cultural hub of China, but also the greatest international metropolis, and hence the title "thoroughfare of the world".

During its long history, Kaifeng has been celebrated as a marvelous place with rich

resources and outstanding people. The political, economical and cultural development had a tremendous impact not only to the central plain area but also to the whole country. There were many celebrated figures in Kaifeng's long history, such as Cai Yong, Cai Wenji, Cui Hao, etc. The brilliant history gives the city abundant tourist attractions. The replica ancient architectures are built in various distinct styles. Furthermore, there are the Daxiangguo Temple, the Bao Zheng's Memorial Temple, the Yuefei Temple in Zhuxian Town and other scenic and historic sites.

The Bao Zheng's Memorial Temple

Occupying a floorage of about 10 000 m^2 on the bank of Baogong Lake, the Bao Zheng's Memorial Temple was built to commemorate the respectable and morally lofty official Bao Zheng, who is considered as one of the most honest and upright judges in Chinese history. The architecture style is simple and unsophisticated, but solemn and stately.

The Daxiangguo Temple (The Temple of Chief Minister)

Located in the center of Kaifeng, the Daxiangguo Temple is a noted Buddhist temple in China. During the Northern Song Dynasty, it was the biggest shrine in the capital, and also the center for Buddhist activities all over the country.

杭州

Hangzhou

杭州是浙江省的省会，是驰名中外的旅游城市，也是历史文化名城和中国七大古都之一。

杭州历史悠久，文化遗产丰富。早在四五千年前的新石器时代，先民就创造了璀璨的被称为文明曙光的良渚文化。杭州古称钱唐。自秦时设钱唐县治以来，已有2 200多年历史。南宋建炎三年(1129年)，杭州升为临安府。绍兴八年（1138年），南宋正式定都临安，历时140余年。

杭州是中国沿海经济发达地区的重要城市之一，工业以机械、电子、化工、轻工、纺织为支柱。杭州也是中国著名的旅游城市。杭州风景秀丽，与苏州共享"上有天堂，下有苏杭"的美誉。

小故事　Anecdote

西湖的湖心亭上有一块石碑，上面写着"虫二"二字。

当年乾隆皇帝来这里游玩，湖心寺方丈请他题匾，他便写了"虫二"二字，众人莫名其妙，一个划船的老人却猜破谜底。原来"虫二"是繁体字"風月"两字的中心笔画，意思是"风月无边"，老人答"水天一色"正好配成对联。

There is a stone tablet in the Mid-lake Pavilion of the West Lake. On the tablet are written two Chinese characters "虫二".

When Emperor Qianlong (1736–1796 AD) was on a visit to the West Lake, the abbot of the Mid-lake Monastery requested calligraphy from him. Then the emperor wrote down "虫二" which confused everybody. An elderly boatman nearby figured out that "虫二" was the middle strokes of the complicated form of the two characters "風月 (wind and moon, referring to scenery)" meaning the wonders of natural beauty are boundless. The elderly boatman then matched it with "the water merges with the horizon far beyond" to complete the couplet.

<table>
<tr><td>1</td><td>2</td></tr>
</table>

1. 杭州
   Hangzhou City
2. 西湖
   The West Lake

小资料　Data

岳王庙里供奉的是南宋民族英雄岳飞。他率领岳家军屡次打败敌人，但是奸臣秦桧却将他害死。后人为了纪念他，便修建了岳王庙。跪在岳王墓前的四个铁人像就是秦桧等几个奸臣。

The Temple of General Yue Fei is dedicated to Yue Fei (1103–1142 AD), a national hero of the Southern Song Dynasty (1127–1279 AD). He led the Song troops and defeated the enemies many times, until he was betrayed by a treacherous official named Qin Hui (1090–1155 AD, Prime Minister of the Southern Song Dynasty detested as a traitor in Chinese history). People of a later generation built the temple to commemorate Yue Fei. The four iron statues kneeling before the tomb of General Yue stand for Qin Hui and other three treacherous officials.

西湖

西湖是杭州最著名的景区，三面环山，山水秀丽，景色迷人，文物古迹非常多。

湖中有三座石塔，称为"三潭"，塔身为球形，中间是空心，夜晚塔中点上蜡烛，烛光倒映在湖面上像一个个小月亮，因此人们称之为"三潭印月"。

六和塔

六和塔建于970年，塔高59.89米，外观13层，塔内为7层，屹立在钱塘江边。

钱塘江大潮

钱塘江大潮是世界上最大的江海潮。它发生在杭州市东北的海盐县境内，每年农历八月十五至八月十八，在钱塘江入海口处形成特大潮水，非常壮观。

Hangzhou

Hangzhou is the capital of Zhejiang Province. It is a world-famous tourist destination, a city with long history and profound culture, and also one of the seven ancient capitals in China.

Hangzhou has a long history, and extensive cultural heritages. As early as in the New Stone Age, 4 000 to 5 000 years ago, its first inhabitants created the splendid Liangzhu Culture, reputedly called the twilight of civilization. Hangzhou was called Qiantang in ancient times. Over 2 200 years has passed since it was designated as the seat of Qiantang County in the Qin Dynasty. In 1129, Hangzhou was renamed Lin'an. In 1138, the Southern Song Dynasty made Lin'an (which stood in present-day Hangzhou) its capital, and since then it served as the capital in the following 140 years.

Hangzhou is an important city in China's coastal areas which are developed and wealthy in the country. Machinery, electronics, chemical engineering, light industry and textiles are the backbone of Hangzhou's industry. Hangzhou is also a famous tourist city in China. With its beautiful scenery, it shares with Suzhou the reputation of "the paradise of the world".

The West Lake

The West Lake is the most famous tourist spot in Hangzhou. Surrounded by graceful mountains on three sides, it has charming scenery and many cultural relics and historic sites.

There are three stone pagodas in the middle of the lake. The main body of the pagodas is the shape of a ball and hollow inside. At night, candles are lit in the pagodas, and their reflections on the lake look like many small moons, hence the name "Three Pools Mirroring the Moon".

The Six-Harmony Pagoda

Built in 970 AD, the Six-Harmony Pagoda, 59.89 m tall, stands by the Qiantang River. Viewed from outside, it has 13 floors, however, inside the pagoda, it only has seven floors.

The Bore of the Qiantang River

The bore of the Qiantang River is the most powerful river bore in the world. It occurs in Haiyan County to the northeast of Hangzhou City. Every year from August 15 to 18 in the Lunar Calendar, the spectacular high tidal waves rush to the narrow estuary where the Qiantang River flows into the sea.

▶ 小知识 Knowledge

杭州气候温和，四季分明，物产丰富，特别是这里的丝绸非常著名，深受中外游人的喜爱。

Hangzhou has mild climate and clear distinction between the four seasons. It is rich in products. The locally produced silk is especially treasured by visitors both at home and abroad.

安阳

Anyang

安阳早在公元前14世纪就被定为都城。当时，商代的第20代国王盘庚把国都迁于殷（今河南安阳小屯村）。商代统治者大兴土木，使殷成为一座古代大都。商代以后，中原王朝曾多次建都于安阳，但在城市建设上没有什么成就。由于战乱，这座古城早已成为废墟。宋代以后，这里不断发现殷代文化和建筑遗存，特别是新中国成立后，经几次大的发掘，基本弄清了城市的规模和布局，人们把这些城市建筑遗迹称为殷墟。

殷墟位于洹水之滨，距现在的安阳1千米，东西最宽处10千米，南北最宽处5千米，总面积24平方千米以上，在这片地域中，共发现宫室建筑遗址50余处。

殷墟甲骨文
Inscriptions on tortoise shells in Yinxu

从殷墟现存的遗迹来看，这座古都已经表现了城市建筑方面较成熟的水平。宫室、民居、作坊、墓地的规划已经比较完善了。宫室建筑高大、豪华，最大的房屋达到400平方米，房基夯土厚达2米。这些都说明，殷墟在当时已是一座规划完整，布局清晰，建筑水平较高的古代都城。

目前，安阳已经成为河南省的一座重要城市，每年都有不少专家、学者前去考察，并吸引着大批游人前往游览。

Anyang

河南安阳出土文物
The cultural relic excavated in Anyang

Anyang was designated as a capital as early as the 14th century BC, when the 20th king of the Shang Dynasty, Pangeng, moved the capital to Yin (today's Xiaotun village, Anyang City, Henan province).

The rulers of the Shang Dynasty organized an immense construction there, and finally built Yin into a great capital in ancient China. After that, some other kingdoms in the Central Plains (comprising the middle and lower reaches of the Yellow River) also chose Anyang as the capital as well, but no further accomplishment with regard to city construction was made. This ancient city was reduced to ruins by countless wars. After the Song Dynasty, cultural and architectural relics of the Yin times were discovered from time to time, especially in several large-scale excavations after the founding of People's Republic of China. Gradually the scale and layout of the ancient city have become more and more clear. Today the architecture ruins of the city are called "Yinxu (the Ruins of Yin)" .

Lying about one kilometer away from Anyang, the Shang Dynasty Ruins (Yinxu) spread to both banks of the Huanhe River. In latitudinal direction, the longest distance of the ruins is about 10 km, while in longitudinal direction, the longest distance is about 5 km. It has an area of more than 24 km^2, and in this area, more than 50 palace ruins have been found.

Viewed from the extant Yinxu ruins, this ancient city demonstrated a relatively high level in constructing city architecture. The layout of the palaces, folk houses, workshops, and graveyards was fairly mature. The palaces are grand and luxurious. The area of the largest palace is up to 400 m^2, and the base earth is up to 2 m thick. All these indicate that Yinxu was a mature ancient capital with an integrated plan, clear layout and high level of architecturual skills in that period.

Today, Anyang has become an important city in Henan province. Every year it attracts many scholars and experts for archaeological research, and large number of tourists.

魅力城市
Enchanting Cities

上海

Shanghai

Shanghai

上海位于长江入海口，是中国最大的城市之一，同时也是一座历史文化名城和著名的旅游城市。上海是中国最大的经济中心，是全国最重要的工业基地，也是重要的贸易、金融和文化中心。

在古代，上海就曾经是贸易港口、全国最大的棉织业中心、贸易大港和漕粮运输中心，被称为"江海之通津，东南之都会"。鸦片战争以后，上海辟为通商口岸，工业、经济发展迅速，曾被称为"冒险家的乐园"。"两千年历史看西安，一千年历史看北京，一百年历史看上海"。上海是近现代中国的"缩影"。

今日的上海，交通四通八达，是中国最大港口、华东地区最大的交通枢纽，沪宁、沪杭两条铁路干线的起点，又是中国重要航空中心和国际航空港之一。这里有发达的商业，是中国特大型综合性贸易中心和国际经济、金融、贸易中心之一。

上海文教科学技术基础雄厚，集中了50多所全日制高等院校，拥有800多所科研机构，55万科技人员，是中国工业科技最大的基地之一。

上海具有中西交融的独特气质，极具现代化而又不失中国传统特色。在上海，有外滩

外滩

外滩是上海最著名的旅游景点之一。外滩建筑风格多样，有古代的、现代的，有中国的和外国的，享有"万国建筑博览会"之美誉。

豫园

豫园位于上海市黄浦区，是著名的江南古典园林。豫园围墙上缀有五条巨龙，龙身用瓦片砌成，五条巨龙形态各异，非常好看。

老式的西洋建筑，也有浦东现代的摩天大厦；有徐家汇大教堂，也有玉佛寺。在这里，沪剧、滑稽戏和交响乐、芭蕾舞同时被人们所欣赏，大家可以品尝本帮佳肴、各地小吃，也可以吃到法国人菜、美式快餐。

东方明珠电视塔

东方明珠电视塔，矗立在黄浦江边，塔高 468 米，是目前世界第三、亚洲第一高塔。

1 | 2

1. 上海
   Shanghai City
2. 杨浦大桥
   Yangpu Bridge

Shanghai

Located on the estuary of the Yangtze River, Shanghai is not only one of the largest cities in China but also a famous city of history, culture and tourism. It is the biggest economic center and the most important industrial base in China. It also flourishes as a hub of trade, finance and culture.

In ancient times, Shanghai was a big trading port, the largest textile center in the country,

and the center for transporting grain to the capital. People used to say Shanghai was the "port connecting rivers and oceans, and the capital of the southeast China". After the Opium Wars, Shanghai was opened to the West as a trading

port. The development of industry and commerce gave Shanghai a reputation as a city for adventurers. It is said that Xi'an reflects China's history of 2 000 years, while Beijing mirrors its history of 1 000 years. To know China's history in the latest 100 years, you'd better look at Shanghai—the epitome of modern and contemporary China.

Shanghai now has transport lines extending in all directions. It is the largest port in China, the largest transportation hub in East China, the starting point of the Huning (Shanghai-Nanjing) and Huhang (Shanghai-Hangzhou) railways, an important aviation

center of China, and one of the international aviation ports. With its advanced commerce, Shanghai is a super large comprehensive trading center in China, and one of the international economic, financial and trading centers.

Shanghai has a solid foundation of culture, education, science and technology. It boasts over 50 colleges and universities, more than 800 research organizations and 550 000 scientific researchers. It is the largest base of industrial science and technology in China.

Shanghai has a unique atmosphere through the mixture of West and East, old and new. In Shanghai, the western buildings of the Bund retain much of their previous grandeur, while the skyscrapers in Pudong are just as spectacular. There are also the Xujiahui Cathedral and the Jade Buddha Temple. Here the Hu (Shanghai) Opera, farces, the symphony and the ballet can be equally appreciated and accepted. People can not only taste local dishes and delicacies from all across China, but also enjoy French cuisine and American fast food.

The Oriental Pearl TV Tower

The Oriental Pearl TV Tower, Standing by the Huangpu River, is 468 m high. It is the third tallest tower in the world and the tallest in Asia.

The Bund

The Bund is the most famous scenic spot in Shanghai where one can see various styles of architecture, including classical and modern, domestic and foreign styles, hence reputed to be "architectural exposition of all countries in the world".

The Yuyuan Garden

The Yuyuan Garden, located in the Huangpu District, is a famous classical garden in Jiangnan (the area south of the Yangtze River). Its walls are decorated with five huge dragons made of tiles. Varied in shape and posture, the five dragons look magnificent.

2 | 1. 上海夜景
1 | Shanghai at night
2. 豫园
Yuyuan Garden

广州

Guangzhou

广州是广东省省会，是重要的历史文化名城和华南经济中心。

广州市靠近南海，夏季并不酷热，冬季暖湿，四季百花开放，又有花城的称号。

广州是中国南方重要的交通枢纽。这里是海港、河港兼具的综合性港口，也是京广（北京至广州）、广九（广州至九龙）铁路的交会点。白云机场设备先进，有班机通往国内和国际各个重要的城市。

广州是对外开放的一个城市，是对外贸易的重要基地。自1957年开始，每年举行两次出口商品交易会。

广州风景优美，有白云山、越秀山、从化温泉等著名景点。广州又是对外科技文化

交流的重要场所。市内有中山大学、暨南大学、华南师范大学和华南植物园、科学院等众多科研机构。

越秀公园

越秀公园是广州最大的公园。园内有镇海楼、五羊雕塑、人工湖和许多亭台楼阁及纪念性建筑物。

镇海楼建于明初，高 28 米，呈长方形，是广州的著名古迹。

光孝寺

光孝寺是广东省最古老的建筑之一。寺内有东、西两座千佛铁塔。其中，西塔建于 963 年，是中国现存的最古老的铁塔。

2	1. 广州市容
1	A glimpse of Guangzhou City
	2. 五羊雕像
	The five-goat statue

▶ 小资料　Data

广州城始建于秦，名"番禺城"，三国时称为广州州治，这就是"广州"名称的开始。到了唐代这里已经是世界著名的商港。宋代时广州成为中国最大的商业城市和通商口岸，城垣多次扩建。

The city of Guangzhou was originally built in the Qin Dynasty under the name of Panyu City. During the Three Kingdoms (220-280 AD) period, it was the seat of the Guangzhou government. The name of Guangzhou came from this period. By the Tang Dynasty, this place had become a world-famous commercial port. In the Song Dynasty, Guangzhou turned into the largest commercial city and trade port in China. The city wall expanded several times at that time.

Guangzhou

Guangzhou, the capital city of Guangdong Province, is an important historical and cultural city and the economic center of southern China.

Guangzhou City is close to the South China Sea. The summer here is not very hot, while the winter is warm and humid. It has blossoming flowers all year round, so it is also affectionately called the "flower city".

Guangzhou is a pivotal transportation center in south China. It is a port with the dual functions of sea port and river port. It is also where the Jingguang (Beijing-Guangzhou) and Guangjiu (Guangzhou-Jiulong) railways meet. The Baiyun Airport here has first-class facilities and flights that can fly to many major cities both at home and abroad.

Guangzhou adopted the opening up policy, and serves as an important base of international trade. Since 1957, export commodities fair is held twice in the city every year.

Guangzhou has beautiful scenery. Its scenic spots include Baiyun Hill, Yuexiu Hill, the Conghua Hot Spring and so on. Guangzhou is also a significant venue for international communication in science, technology and culture. It boasts many famous universities and research organizations such as Sun Yat-sen University, Jinan University, South China Normal University, the South China Botanic Garden, and the Academy of Science.

Yuexiu Park

Yuexiu Park is the largest park in Guangzhou. There are the Zhenhai (guarding the Sea) Tower, the Five-Goat Sculpture and a number of constructions such as man-made lakes, pavilions, towers, verandas, as well as memorial buildings.

The Zhenhai (guarding the Sea) Tower was built in the early Ming Dynasty (1368 — 1644 AD). It is 28 m high, in rectangular shape. It is a noted historical site in Guangzhou.

The Temple of Honor and Filial Piety

The Temple of Honor and Filial Piety is one of the oldest buildings in Guangdong Province. In the temple there are eastern and western iron towers of one thousand Buddhas. The western tower was built in 963 AD. It is the oldest iron tower extant in China.

1. 中山纪念堂
   Sun Yat-Sen Memorial Hall
2. 白云山
   The Baiyun Hill

1 | 2

▶ 你知道吗？ Do you know?

广州别称"羊城"，简称"穗"。

相传曾经有五位仙人骑着口含谷穗的羊降临广州，祝愿此地"永无荒饥"。仙人隐去后，五羊化为石像，从此广州得名"羊城"。广州自宋代开始就有羊城八景的评选。自宋以后，评选羊城八景成了传统，历代相沿，从不间断。

Guangzhou is also called "City of Goats" or "Sui" for short.

It is said that once five immortals arrived in Guangzhou riding goats whose mouth holding ears of wheat. The immortals prayed that there would be no starvation in the place. They then disappeared, and the five goats changed into stone statues. Guangzhou was called the City of Goats hereafter. Guangzhou started the activity of selecting eight scenic spots of the City of Goats in the Song Dynasty. This activity has become a tradition ever since then, passing down from generation to generation.

深圳

Shenzhen

深圳夜景
Shenzhen at night

深圳是中国设立最早的经济特区之一。改革开放以来，发展迅速，现已成为经济发达的现代化都市。

自从改革开放以来，深圳从沿海的一个小渔村，逐步成为工商、农牧、住宅、旅游等综合发展的新兴现代化城市。

20世纪90年代以后，高新技术产业迅速发展。财政收入与进出口总额均位居全国前列。

深圳是改革开放的窗口，吸收了各地传统文化。独特的环境，使深圳成为一个适合创业的城市。深圳也关注城市的自然生态，这是一个美丽的花

小资料 Data

早在 6700 多年前的新石器时代中期，就有土著先民生活在深圳。秦始皇统一中国后，深圳隶属于南海郡。"深圳" 地名在史籍中最早的记载是 1410 年。深圳因为水泽密布、村落边有一条深水沟而得名。

6 700 years ago, in the middle of the New Stone Age, this place was inhabited by some aboriginals. After emperor Qinshihuang of the Qin Dynasty unified China, Shenzhen was subordinate to Nanhai Prefecture. The name Shenzhen can be traced back to 1410 AD according to historical records. The name Shenzhen ("deep ditch"in Chinese) derives from its location:it abounds in pools and there is a deep gully beside the village.

园城市，向世界展示着它特有的活力与希望。

大鹏古城

大鹏古城是国家级文物保护单位，位于龙岗区大鹏镇鹏城村。它建于明洪武二十七年，历经 600 多年风雨仍巍然屹立。深圳又称鹏城。

锦绣中华微缩景区

锦绣中华微缩景区是世界上面积最大、内容最丰富的微缩景区，拥有万里长城、秦始皇兵马俑坑、北京故宫、杭州西湖、长江三峡、苏州园林等微缩景观。

中国民俗文化村

中国民俗文化村是中国第一个集各民族民间艺术、民俗风情和民居建筑于一园的大型文化旅游景区，有 "中国民俗博物馆" 之美誉。游客在村寨里可以欣赏和参与各民族的歌舞表演，也可参与制作工艺品和民族风味食品。

你知道吗？ Do you know?

中国还有哪几个经济特区？
继深圳后，中国又相继成立了 4 个经济特区：珠海经济特区、厦门经济特区、汕头经济特区和海南经济特区。

What are the other SEZs in China?
China established four Special Economic Zones successively after Shenzhen. They are Zhuhai, Xiamen, Shantou, and Hainan SEZs.

Shenzhen

Shenzhen is one of the first special economic zones (SEZ) in China. After the reform and opening up, it grew fast and now has become a modernized metropolis with a flourishing economy.

With a modest origin as a tiny fishing village, Shenzhen, one of the first cities to "open" with the economic reforms, has miraculously become a new modern city which developed in an all-around way in the areas of industry and commerce, agriculture and husbandry and real estate and tourism. Since the 1990s, its high-tech industry has developed rapidly. Its revenue and the total amount of exports and imports rank among the best ones in the country.

Shenzhen is a show-case for China's reform and openning-up. It absorbs the traditions and cultures from all across the country. Its unique environment enables Shenzhen to be a pioneering city in China. Shenzhen also attaches significance to the natural ecology of the city. This beautiful garden city is demonstrating its unique vitality and future to the whole world.

The Dapeng Old City

The Dapeng Old City is a relic under state protection. It is located in the Pengcheng village of Dapeng town, Long-gang district. It was built in the 27th year of Hongwu in the Ming Dynasty, and still stands erect after six hundred years. Shenzhen is also called the "Peng (roc) City".

The Micro-Scenic Spot of Charming and Beautiful China

The Micro-Scenic Spot of Charming and Beautiful China is the largest micro-scenic spot with the most substantial content in the world. It gathers a large number of tourist attractions from all corners of China in miniature, including such scenic and historical sites as the Great Wall, the Terracotta Warriors and Horses of Emperor Qinshihuang, the Palace Museum of Beijing, the West Lake of Hangzhou, the Three Gorges of the Yangtze River, the Gardens of Suzhou, etc.

The Village of Chinese Folk Customs and Culture

The Village of Chinese Folk Customs and Culture is the first large-scale cultural tourist spot packing folk arts, folk customs and residential buildings of all ethnic minorities into one park in China. It is called "the Chinese folk customs museum". Tourists can enjoy and even partake in not only the singing and dancing of every nationality in the villages but also producing artworks and cooking foods with ethnic flavors.

1 | 2　1. 民俗文化村
　　　The Village of Chinese Folk
　　　Customs and Culture
　　2. 世界之窗
　　　Window of the World

昆明

Kunming

昆明是云南省省会，是重要的工业城市，还是中国西南门户、历史文化名城和对外开放城市。

昆明自然风光优美，气候四季如春，鲜花长开不谢，"天气常如二三月，花枝不断四时春"，享有"春城"和"花都"的美誉。但是，昆明昼夜和晴雨之间的温差较大，又有"四季无寒暑，一雨便成冬"的说法。

昆明是一座历史悠久的多民族边疆文化名城和世界

著名的旅游城市。市内有许多名胜古迹和风景区，主要有大观楼、圆通寺、铜瓦寺、古代航海家郑和故里、著名音乐家聂耳墓等。著名风景游览区有西山、滇池、昆明植物园等。

大观楼

大观楼坐落在滇池边，高三层，呈方形，红墙绿瓦。登楼远眺，海阔天空，湖光山色，尽收眼底。楼前的一幅180字长联被誉为古今第一长联。

世界园艺博览园场馆

昆明世界园艺博览园场馆是一组较为宏大的建筑群，占地218万平方米，主要有国际馆、中国馆、人与自然馆、大温室、科技馆等建筑。国际馆建筑面积12 006平方米，由一圆形主体和100多米长的弧形墙组成。中国馆占地约20 000平方米，是世博会最大的室内展馆，用于展示绚丽多彩的中国园林园艺。

▶ 小资料 Data

"昆明"一名始于1271年。1276年设置云南行中书省，设昆明县。1931年改为昆明市，抗日战争时期是中国后方重要城镇。

The name "Kunming" can be traced back to 1271 AD. In 1276 the province of Yunnan was set up, and Kunming County was established. In 1931, Kunming became a city. It was an important city in the rear area during the period of the Resistance War against Japan (1937—1945).

▶ 小资料 Data

1999年5月在昆明举办的世界园艺博览会，使昆明的知名度空前提高，是昆明全方位走向世界的重要里程碑，对昆明乃至云南扩大对外开放，加快经济发展和社会全面进步都有深远的影响。

The Kunming International Horticultural Expo was held in May 1999. It made Kunming more prominent and was a significant milestone in the opening of the city to the world. It has had a far-reaching impact in creating more room for reform and opening up, speeding up economic development and developing a progressive society not only in Kunming but also in Yunnan Province.

2 1. 昆明市容
1   A glimpse of Kunming City
   2. 滇池风光
      The Dianchi Lake

Kunming

Kunming, the capital of Yunnan Province, is an important industrial city and the gateway of Southwest China. It is also a famous city with long history and extensive culture, and a city open to the world.

Kunming has beautiful natural scenery. Its four seasons are all like spring, and flowers blossom all year round. A poem describes the weather here as "the climate is constantly similar to that in February and March, the flowers never cease to blossom, and the four seasons are all spring". So Kunming enjoys the reputation of being a "spring city" and "flower city". However, there is a big difference in temperature between day and night, and between sunny days and rainy days. As the saying goes, "there are no differences between winters and summers, but winter comes after rain".

With a long history, Kunming is a famous city in the border area where many ethnic groups coexist. There are a lot of cultural relics and scenic spots in Kunming, which has become a famous international tourist city. The historical sites include the Grand View Tower, the Yuantong Temple, the Tongwa Temple, the birthplace of Zheng He (a famous explorer of sea in the history), and the tomb of Nie Er (a famous musician). The noted scenic spots include the West Mountain, Dianchi Lake, the Kunming Botanical Garden and so on.

The Grand View Tower

The Grand View Tower, located by Dianchi Lake, is a three-storey square building. It has red walls and green tiles. From the tower one has a panoramic view of the boundless sky, the beautiful lake and mountains. The long couplet with 180 Chinese characters here is reputed to be the longest couplet in ancient and modern times.

The Kunming International Horticultural Expo Site

The Kunming International Horticultural Expo Site is a group of magnificent buildings, covering an area of 2 180 000 m^2, including the International Stadium, the China Stadium, the Stadium of Human and Nature, the Great Greenhouse, the Science Stadium, etc. The International Stadium, with a floor space of 12 006 m^2, is made up of a round main building and has a long arc wall over 100 m long. The China Stadium, covering an area of about 20 000 m^2, is the largest indoor stadium in the Expo and is used to display the wonders of Chinese gardening.

世界园艺博览园
Kunming International Horticultural Expo Site

苏州

Suzhou

　　苏州位于江苏省南部，是中国历史文化名城和著名园林风景城市，简称苏，也叫姑苏。

　　苏州古典园林最盛的时候有大小园林 250 余座。这里的园林最著名的有宋代的沧浪亭，元代的狮子林，明代的拙政园，清代的网师园、留园及西园。其中拙政园和留园与北京颐和园、承德避暑山庄合称中国四大园林。苏州西郊枫桥寒山寺是著名的古代寺院，唐代诗人张继的《枫桥夜泊》里有一句就说到"姑苏城外寒山寺"。

　　苏州的文化事业历来都很发达，文物收藏非常丰富，旅游事业发展迅速。苏州是一个文雅秀美的历史名城，吸引着八方来客。

而得名。

拙政园

　　拙政园建于明朝，全园分为东园、中园、西园三部分。

　　中园是拙政园的精华部分，其总体布局以水池为中心，亭台楼榭临水而建，有的亭榭则直接从水中冒出来，具有江南水乡的特色。

沧浪亭

　　沧浪亭是苏州最古老的一所名园，为宋代诗人苏子美所筑。园内以假山为主，山上古木参天，著名的沧浪亭就隐蔽其中。

狮子林

　　狮子林是元代园林的代表。它以太湖石堆砌的精巧假山而著称，很多石峰形状像狮子，千姿百态，栩栩如生，因

留园

　　留园具有清代园林的风格。它以水池为中心：池南的涵碧山房与明瑟楼是其主体建筑；池北多为假山小亭，林木交映；池西假山上的闻木樨香轩，是俯视全园景色最佳处，并有长廊与各处相通；池东以曲院回廊见胜，有三座石峰，中间为冠云峰，高6.5米，是江南最大的太湖石。

Suzhou

Suzhou, located in the south of Jiangsu Province, is a famous historical and cultural city with many beautiful ancient gardens. It is called "Su" for short, and also called "Gusu".

Suzhou once had over 250 classical gardens, big or small, during its gold age. The most noted gardens here include the Canglangting Garden of the Song Dynasty, the Lion Garden of the Yuan Dynasty, the Humble Administrator's Garden of the Ming Dynasty, the Wangshi Garden, the Liuyuan Garden and the West Garden of the Qing Dynasty. The Humble Administrator's Garden and the Liuyuan Garden, together with Beijing's Summer Palace and the Chengde Summer resort, are called the four great gardens of China. Hanshan Temple, located in the west outskirts of Suzhou, is a famous ancient temple. The poem of "A Night Mooring by Maple Bridge" by Zhang Ji, a famous poet of the Tang Dynasty, mentioned "the Hanshan Temple outside the Gusu City".

Suzhou has always been a well developed city of culture, with a rich collection of cultural relics. Its tourism has developed quickly. This elegant historical city attracts visitors from all around the world.

The Canglangting Garden
The Canglangting Garden is the

▶ 小知识 Knowledge

园林之城的苏州有"江南园林甲天下，苏州园林甲江南"之说。1997年12月，苏州古典园林被联合国教科文组织列入世界文化遗产名录。

As the Chinese saying goes, "Gardens in Jiangnan are the finest in China, while gardens in Suzhou are the best in Jiangnan". In December 1997 the classical gardens of Suzhou was listed as a world cultural heritage site by UNESCO.

oldest famous garden in Suzhou. Built by Su Zimei, a poet in the Song Dynasty, the garden is centered on artificial hills covered with lush ancient trees. The famous Canglang Pavilion is hidden among the trees.

The Lion Garden

The Lion Garden is representative of the gardens of the Yuan Dynasty (1206 — 1368 AD). It excels in artificial hills piled by rocks from the Taihu Lake. Many of the rocks look like vivid lions in various postures, hence its name.

The Humble Administrator's Garden

The Humble Administrator's Garden, built in the Ming Dynasty, is divided into three parts — the eastern, middle and western gardens.

The middle one is the most essential part of the entire garden. With a pool in the center, the architect designed pavilions, terraces and buildings near the water, some of which poping out from the water directly. It is characteristic of the Jiangnan (south of the lower reaches of the Yangtze River) Style.

The Liuyuan Garden

The Liuyuan Garden has the style of the gardens of the Qing Dynasty. It takes the pool as the center, while the Hill House of Containing Green and the Building of Bright Zither to the south of the pool are the main buildings; north of the pool are artificial hills and pavilions amid trees; west of the lake, the Veranda of Smelling Sweet-scented Osmanthus on an artificial hill is the best spot to overlook the whole garden. The Veranda is connected with other places by promenades. The eastern side of the pool is characterized by winding courtyards and corridors dominated by three large pieces of rockwork. The middle one is called Cloud-Capped Rock. It is about 6.5 m high and is the biggest rock from the Taihu Lake in the Jiangnan area.

青岛

Qingdao

青岛是中国对外开放港口，是山东省综合性工业城市，又是著名的疗养、避暑及游览胜地。

青岛市内街道和建筑依山势起伏，整洁优美。市内游览区很多，栈桥是青岛的象征，它的入海尽头建有"回澜阁"。老城区至今仍具有浓郁的欧陆情调，建筑大部分是20世纪初期德国人建的，教堂、别墅等老房子形成"红瓦绿树、碧海蓝天"的独特景观。市郊东北部是崂山山脉，主峰海拔1 133米，是中国名山之一，山里有很多名胜古迹。

Qingdao

1 青岛的海滨
  A beach in Qingdao City
2. 青岛的街道
  A street scene in Qingdao City

▶ 小资料 Data

青岛因离海岸不远处有一小岛叫"青岛"而得名，原来是渔村，清朝以来贸易逐渐兴盛。曾经被德国强行租借，成为商港和军港，又两度被日本强占，1949年6月2日解放。

Qingdao is named after a small island called Qingdao (Green Island) not far from its coast. It was originally a small fishing village. Then the commerce there gradually throve in the Qing Dynasty. When Germany forced the Qing government to lease Qingdao to Germany, Qingdao was ceded to become a commercial and military port. It was occupied twice by Japan afterwards. On June 2, 1949, it was liberated.

As a comprehensive industrial city in Shandong province, Qingdao is one of China's trading ports to the outside world. It is also a noted convalescent and summer resort.

The streets and buildings in Qingdao are shipshape, rising and falling based on the topographic undulation. There are many scenic spots in the city. The dock Zhanqiao (trestle) Bridge is Qingdao's symbol, with the Huilan Pavilion at its end extending out to the sea. Nowadays, the old districts in the city still have European style and sentiments. Most of architecture was built by Germans in the early 20th century. Some old buildings, like the churches and villas, form a unique sight of "red tiles, green trees, jade sea and blue sky". The Laoshan Mountain Range, in the northeast of the suburbs, is one of the famous mountains in China. There are many scenic spots in the mountain range. The highest peak of the range is 1 133 m high.

大连

Dalian

　　大连在辽宁省，是中国北方著名港口和工业、旅游城市。

　　大连工业基础雄厚，是中国重要工业基地之一，又是综合性工业城市。这里是重要的渔业基地，水产资源丰富。大连港是中国主要外贸口岸，大连国际机场有通往中国重要城市的航班。

　　大连是中国首批优秀旅游城市。大连有多处海水浴场，老虎滩公园有全长600米的中国第一条跨海游览客运索道。

1 | 2

1. 劳动公园
   Laodong Park

2. 金石滩
   Jinshi Beach

Dalian

Located in Liaoning Province, Dalian is a famous port in the northern China and also a well-known industrial and tourist city.

Dalian has a solid industrial foundation, and is one of the important industrial bases in China. With abundant aquatic resources, it is also an important fishery base. Dalian is a major port for international trade in China. Its international airport has airlines to every major city in China.

Dalian is at the top of the list of excellent tourist cities in China. There are several beaches for swimmers in the city. The Tiger Beach Park is the first in China to have built a tourist cableway across the gulf with a length of 600 m.

▶ **小资料** Data

大连每年举行国际服装节、商品进出口交易会、烟花爆竹迎春会、赏槐会、国际马拉松赛、冰峪冰灯会等大型活动，还成功举办了 1997 中国旅游交易会和第二届中国花卉交易会。大连国际马拉松赛也已经成功地举办了 20 届。

Every year Dalian hosts many grand festivals, such as the International Fashion Festival, the Import & Export Trade Fair, the Spring Firecracker Festival, the Pagoda Trees Appreciation Festival, the International Marathon Tournament, and the "Bingyu" (Ice Valley) Ice Lantern Festival. It successfully held the Travel & Tourist Trade Fair in 1997 and the Second Chinese Flowers Trade Fair. Dalian International Marathon Tournament has been successfully hosted there for 20 times.

▶ **你知道吗？** Do you know?

大连的广场星罗棋布。海之韵广场、胜利广场、 中山广场、人民广场、奥林匹克广场……有资料显示的大连广场约 70 个左右。大连可能是亚洲拥有广场最多的城市。广场丰富了大连文化，展示了城市的迷人魅力。

Dalian city is decorated with many pretty squares, such as the Haizhiyun Square (Sea Rhyme Square), the Triumph Square, the Sun Yat-sen Square, the Renmin Square (People's Square), the Olympic Square, etc. Statistics show that there are about 70 squares in the city. Dalian probably has the largest number of squares in Asia. These squares help to enrich the city's culture and demonstrate its charms.

拉萨

Lhasa

布达拉宫
Potala Palace

拉萨位于西藏自治区中部，是西藏自治区首府，西藏政治、经济、文化、宗教及交通中心。她是一座具有1 300多年历史的高原古城，于1951年和平解放。拉萨地处青藏高原，海拔3 500米左右。全年光照充足，有"日光城"之称。

虽然青藏高原的海拔让初来者感到晕眩，但明净壮美的高原风光让人沉醉，千年的历史留下的文化遗迹以及宗教氛围也带给人们巨大的震撼。拉萨名胜古迹众多，布达拉宫、大昭寺等早已驰名中外，还有藏王陵、楚布寺、曲贡遗址、西藏革命展览馆及小昭寺等。

布达拉宫

布达拉宫建筑宏伟，宫墙全部用花岗岩砌筑，是举世闻名的宫堡式建筑群。宫体主楼为13层，高117米，现已被联合国教科文组织列入世界文化遗产名录。

布达拉宫有5座达赖喇嘛的灵塔，其中十三世达赖的灵塔最高，耗用18 870两黄金包裹，上面镶嵌着各种珠宝。殿内的十三世达赖银像是用1 006两白银铸成的。

大昭寺

大昭寺位于拉萨市中心，建于公元7世纪，是藏王松赞干布为纪念唐朝文成公主入藏而建的第一座庙宇。

大昭寺以建筑精美、壁画生动而闻名，是西藏的佛教朝拜圣地。

▶ 你知道吗？ Do you know?

641年，吐蕃部族首领松赞干布完成统一大业后，迎娶唐朝文成公主。公主进藏后建议用白山羊背土填湖建庙。于是，人们称最初的寺庙，即现在的大昭寺为"惹萨"，藏语的意思是"山羊背上"。后来"惹萨"被译成了"逻些"，逐步变成为"拉萨"了。上千年来，这里几度成为西藏政教活动中心，成为名副其实的"神圣之地"。

In 641 AD, Songtsen Gampe, the Chieftain of Tubo having unified the whole Tibetan region, wedded Princess Wencheng of the Imperial Tang Court. After the princess arrived, she suggested building a temple with earth carried by a white goat and filled in the lake. Therefore people called the original temple (the present day Jokhang Temple)"Resa", meaning "goat carrying earth"in Tibetan. Later "Resa"was translated as "Luoxie", and it gradually changed into "Lhasa". In the past thousand years, Lhasa became Tibet's political and religious center several times, and it really matches the name of "the holy place".

Lhasa

Lhasa, the capital of the Tibet Autonomous Region, is situated in the central Tibet. It is the provincial heart of politics, economy, culture, religion and transportation. This ancient city, with a history of over 1 300 years, was liberated peacefully in 1951. With an altitude around 3 500 m, it is located on the Qinghai-Tibet Plateau. The city is sunny all year round, so the city is reputed as a "city of sunshine".

Although newcomers always feel dizzy due to the high altitude on the Qinghai-Tibet Plateau, they will always be inebriated by the bright and grandiose sight on the plateau, and shocked by the cultural relics from thousands of years ago and the awe-inspiring religious atmosphere. Lhasa has many scenic and historical sites, including the famous Potala Palace and Jokhang Temple which are already well-known both at home and abroad. Besides, there are other scenic spots, such as the Tomb of the Tibetan Kings, the Chubu Monastery, the Qugong site, the Tibetan Revolution Exhibition Hall and the Little Jokhang Temple, etc.

The Potala Palace

The magnificent Potala Palace, with its massive granite walls, is a world-famous palatial architecture complex. The main building has 13 storeys and is about 117 m tall. It was inscribed on the world cultural heritage list by UNESCO.

There are five divine stupas of the

Dalai Lamas, among which the stupa for the 13th Dalai Lama is the tallest, being gilded with 943.5 kg of gold and inlaid with various jewels. The 13th Dalai Lama's statue is cast with 50.3 kg of silver.

The Jokhang Temple

The Jokhang Temple, situated in the center of Lhasa, was built in the 7th century and was the first temple built by Songtsen Gampo to commemorate the arrival of Princess Wencheng of the Tang Dynasty. It is famous for its exquisite architecture and vivid mural paintings, and is a holy place for Buddhist pilgrimage in Tibet.

1. 八角街
   Bajiao Street
2. 大昭寺
   Jokhang Temple

香港

Hong Kong

香港是中国进出南海的门户、远东自由港、亚洲和太平洋地区贸易、航运中心和国际金融中心之一。香港包括香港岛、九龙半岛、新界及其附近地区的岛屿。位于香港岛和九龙半岛之间的维多利亚湾，是与美国旧金山、巴西里约热内卢相媲美的世界三大天然良港之一。优越的地理位置和良好的港口使香港成为亚洲水运中心。

香港是亚洲仅次于日本东京的第2大航空港。位于赤鱲角的香港国际机场，可供巨型飞机升降，日夜通

▶ 小资料　Data

公元前 4000 年左右，已有中国先民在香港居住。唐代时中国军队已驻守在这里。1842 年英国逼迫清政府签订了《南京条约》割让香港岛。1860 年签订《北京条约》割让九龙半岛界限街以南的部分（即九龙）。中国政府在 1997 年 7 月 1 日恢复对香港行使主权，设立中华人民共和国香港特别行政区。

Around 4000 BC, Chinese ancestors had already inhabited Hong Kong. Chinese troops were stationed there in the Tang Dynasty. In 1842, Great Britain forced the Qing government to sign the Treaty of Nanjing,ceding Hong Kong Island to Britain. In 1860, the Treaty of Beijing was signed to cede Kowloon, south of the boundary street in Kowloon peninsula. On July 1, 1997, the Chinese government resumed sovereignty over Hong Kong and established the PRC's Hong Kong Special Administrative Region.

航，平均每 5 分钟就有 1 架飞机起飞或降落，是世界上最繁忙的机场之一。

香港与纽约、伦敦、苏黎世同为世界重要的黄金市场和金融中心。金融业在香港被称为百业之首，对香港甚至亚洲各国经济发展起着重要作用。

香港旅游业相当发达，被称为"购物天堂"、"美食之都"，旅游是外汇收入的第三来源。越来越多的香港人外出旅游，主要去中国内地。

香港的娱乐业与电影工业特别发达。动作片，就是香港地区为世界电影贡献的独具魅力的电影类型，成龙等香港演员也成为了世界级巨星。

2 1. 维多利亚湾
　　Victoria Harbor
1 2. 青马大桥
　　Tsing Ma Bridge

Hong Kong

Hong Kong is China's gateway to the South China Sea. It is a free port in the Far East, a trade and shipping center of Asia and Pacific region, and also one of the world's financial centers. Hong Kong falls into Hong Kong Island, Kowloon, the New Territories and the outlying islands. The bustling Victoria Harbor between Hong Kong Island and the Kowloon peninsula is one of the three fine natural harbors in the world(the other two being San Francisco in the U.S. and Rio de Janeiro in the Brazil). Superior geographic position and good harbors make Hong Kong the shipping center of Asia.

Hong Kong airport is the second largest aviation port in Asia, next to that of Tokyo in Japan. The Hong Kong International Airport on Chek Lap Kok Island is well designed to accommodate large aircrafts taking off and landing day and night. It is

one of the busiest airports in the world. Every 5 minutes, there is an airplane taking off or landing.

Hong Kong rivals New York, London and Zurich as the world's most important gold market and financial center. Finance is considered the number one business in Hong Kong, having a great influence on Hong Kong and even the neighboring Asian countries' economic development.

Hong Kong has a well-developed tourism trade. It is called "shoppers' paradise" and "gourmet metropolis". Tourism is the third largest source of foreign exchange income. More and more Hong Kong people go out to travel, and many choose the Chinese mainland as their destination.

Hong Kong's entertainment and movie industries are especially flourishing. Action movies are a unique genre that Hong Kong has contributed to world's movies. Some Hong Kong actors, like Jackie Chan, have become internationally famous big stars.

| 2 | 3 |
| 1 | |

1. 宝莲寺天坛大佛
   The great Buddha of the Temple of Heaven
2. 海洋公园
   The Ocean Park
3. 香港街景
   A street scene in Hong Kong

澳门

Macao

　　澳门位于南海之滨，珠江口西侧，由澳门半岛、凼仔岛和路环岛组成。

　　澳门经济以赌博业（或称博彩业）和旅游业为主。20 世纪60 年代起，澳门经济开始转变，进出口贸易迅猛发展。目前，对外贸易、旅游博彩、建筑业与金融业并列成为澳门经济 4 大支柱。

　　澳门旅游业很兴旺，以妈阁庙、"大三巴"、大炮台最为著名。澳门的赌博业在远东首屈一指，有东方"蒙特卡洛"（东方赌城）的称号。

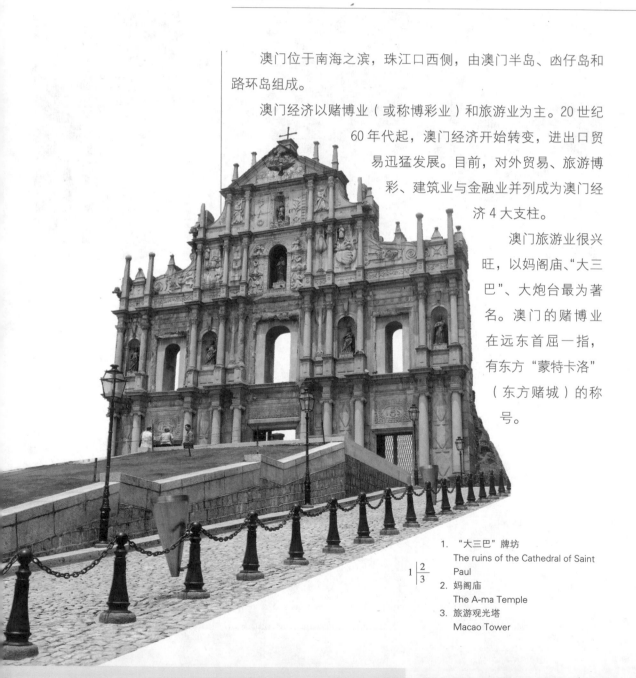

$1\dfrac{2}{3}$

1. "大三巴"牌坊
   The ruins of the Cathedral of Saint Paul
2. 妈阁庙
   The A-ma Temple
3. 旅游观光塔
   Macao Tower

Macao

Macao is situated in the southern coast of South China Sea, to the west of the Pearl River's estuary. It consists of Macao peninsula, the islands of Taipa and Coloane.

Macao's economy relies heavily on tourism and casinos. In the 1960s, Macao reshuffled its economic structure, increasing imports and exports dramatically. At present, foreign trade, tourism and gambling, architecture and banking have become the four pillars of Macao's economy.

Macao's tourism industry is well developed. Its best-known sights are the A-ma Temple, the Cathedral of Saint Paul and the Mount Fortress. The gambling industry in Macao ranks first in the Far East, known as "the Oriental Monte Carlo (a celebrated gambling city in Europe)".

▶ 小资料 Data

澳门自古以来就是中国的领土，原属广东香山县（今中山市）。1553 年葡萄牙人借口曝晒水浸货物，贿赂地方官吏，停靠澳门码头进行贸易。1840 年鸦片战争后，澳门被葡萄牙长期占有。中华人民共和国政府于 1999 年 12 月 20 日对澳门恢复行使主权，设立澳门特别行政区。

Macao has belonged to China since ancient times. It was formerly subordinate to Xiangshan County (today's zhongshan City) of Guangdong Province. In 1553, the Portuguese set foot on Macao on the pretext of drying drenched goods. They bribed local officials to gain permission to drop anchor in Macao's harbor and engage in trade. Since the Opium War in 1840, Macao was occupied by Portuguese for a long time. On December 20th of 1999, the People's Republic of China resumed its sovereignty over Macao and established the Macao Special Administrative Region.

▶ 小知识 Knowledge

圣保罗教堂牌坊（即"大二巴"牌坊）已成为澳门的象征。

The massive stone facade of the ruins of the Cathedral of Saint Paul (Dasanba in Chinese) has become the symbol of Macao.

▶ 你知道吗？ Do you know?

妈阁庙内供奉的是海上保护神——妈祖（闽南语"母亲"的意思），也称"天后"。每年农历除夕和三月廿三日，渔民都来到这里为妈祖祝寿，香火旺盛。

The A-ma Temple is a place to worship the seafarers' goddess "A-ma" (mother in southern Fujian dialect), also known as "the Queen of Heaven". Every year on Chinese New Year's Eve and the 23rd day of the third Chinese Lunar month, fishermen will come here to celebrate A-ma's birthday. There is always an endless stream of pilgrims in the temple.

台北

Taipei

台北市是台湾省最大的城市，是其政治、经济、文化中心，位于台湾岛北部，台北盆地中心。

台北市工商业发达。工业以电机、电器、化工、印刷、纺织等为主。岛内纵贯铁路和南北公路干线建成后，台北成为全岛陆路交通运输中心。

台北市发展历史虽远比台南市晚，但名胜古迹不少。旧台北府城拆除后，留下许多城门；建造于清乾隆三年（1738）的龙山寺是最古老的寺庙，建筑富丽；阳明山游览区范围广阔，与大屯火山群相连，秀丽多姿，其中士林区外双溪故宫博物院，收藏了大量来自北京故宫的珍宝。

台北聚集了台湾省主要高等院校和科研机构，有台湾大学、师范大学、农业试验所、林业试验所等。

Taipei

Taipei, in the north of Taiwan Island and at the center of the Taipei Basin, is the largest city in Taiwan. It is Taiwan's political, economic and cultural center.

Taipei has advanced industry and commerce. Its industry mainly includes electrical machinery, electrical appliance, chemical engineering, printing, textiles and so on. After the longitudinal railways and main highways were built, Taipei became the land transportation hub of the whole island.

Though Taipei's history is shorter than that of Tainan (the ancient provincial capital of Taiwan), it has no less scenic and historic sites. After the old Taipei city was demolished, a lot of city wall gates were left till today. The magnificent Longshan Temple, built in 1738, the third year during Emperor Qianlong's reign in the Qing Dynasty, is the oldest temple in Taiwan. The Yangmingshan Scenic Area, adjoining the Datun Volcanoes, is a large tourist area with its various charming scenic spots. The Shuangxi Palace Museum outside Shilin

1. 台北市容
   A glimpse of Taipei City
2. 台北街景
   A street scene in Taipei

阳明山
The Yangmingshan Hill

district in this area houses a large number of treasures that came from the Forbidden City in Beijing.

Taiwan's main colleges and research organizations are assembled in Taipei, for example, Taiwan University, Normal University, the Institute of Agriculture Research, and the Institute of Forestry Research.

▶ 小资料　Data

台北市的中心区，原名大佳腊。清康熙四十八年（1709），福建人来到这里开垦。1876年置台北府。1895 年，台湾被日本殖民者占有。1945 年 10 月台湾归还祖国。台北为台湾省省会。

The central part of Taipei was originally called Dajiala. In 1709, the 48th year of Emperor Kangxi's reign in the Qing Dynasty, people from Fujian province came here to till the land. In 1876, the Taipei Prefecture was established. The Japanese colonists occupied Taiwan in 1895. In October of 1945, Taiwan was returned to the motherland. Taipei is the capital of Taiwan Province.

中国之旅
Traveling Around China

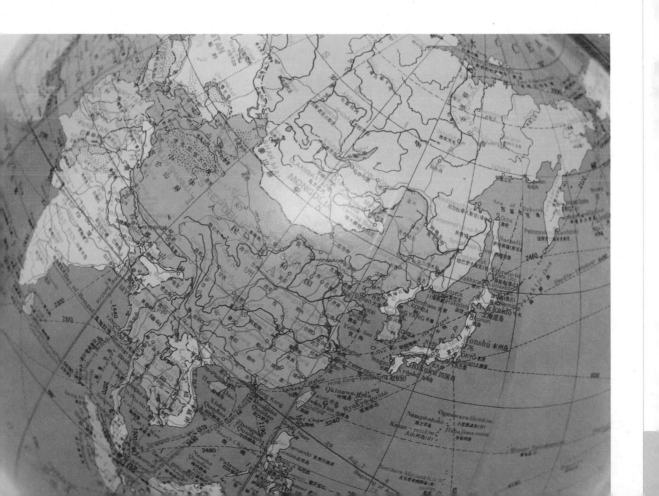

北京故宫

The Palace Museum in Beijing

北京故宫是中国现存规模最大的古建筑群。原来是明、清两代的皇宫，别名紫禁城，又称大内，位居北京城中心。

故宫正门为午门，北面有神武门，东面有东华门，西面有西华门，占地面积72万多平方米，总建筑面积15万平方米，共有房屋9 000余间。周围有城墙，高10米，总长3 440米。四角各有角楼，城外护城河长3 800米，宽52米。

故宫内部由外朝和内廷两大部分组成。外朝三大殿即太和殿、中和殿、保和殿是中心，是皇帝发号施令和举行盛大典礼之处。三大殿的后面部分是内廷，包括后三宫，即乾

太和殿
The Hall of Supreme Harmony

清宫、交泰殿、坤宁宫及东西六宫、御花园等，是皇帝处理政务和皇族居住的地方。

故宫建筑讲究封建等级制度，严格保持对称布局，总体布局体现封建皇权至高无上的地位，以南北为中轴线，重要的前三殿和后三宫自南而北排列在京城中轴线上，采取严格对称的院落式布局，按使用功能分区，不同功能的建筑数目也很有讲究。

故宫内保存有大批珍贵文物，现在成为故宫博物院，这里开辟了宫殿房屋作为宫廷历史遗迹陈列室、青铜器馆、陶瓷馆、明清工艺美术馆、历代艺术馆、珍宝馆等。

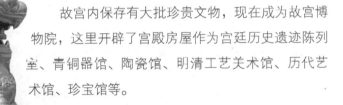

The **Palace Museum** in Beijing

The Palace Museum in Beijing is the largest extant ancient architecture complex in China. Lying in the center of Beijing, it used to be the abode of the Ming and Qing emperors, and was also called the Forbidden City and Danei (the innermost place, namely the imperial palace).

The main entry point for the Palace Museum is the Meridian Gate. It has the Donghua Gate in the east and the Xihua Gate in the west. Enclosed behind its 3 800m-long and 52m-wide moat are more than 9 000 rooms that occupy a floor space of 150 000 m^2 and a total area of over 720 000 m^2. The museum is encircled by 10m-high and 3 400m-long walls. Four corner towers stand majestically at each corner.

The Palace Museum is divided into two parts — the front court and the inner court. The front court is centered on the Hall of Supreme Harmony, the Hall of Central Harmony and the Hall of Preserved Harmony, where the emperor issued edicts and held grand ceremonies. Behind the three halls of the front court is the inner court where the emperor worked and lived with his family and concubines. The inner court comprises the Palace of Celestial Purity, the Palace of Celestial and Terrestrial Union, the Palace of Terrestrial Tranquility, the Imperial Garden and six palaces at the eastern and western sides.

Based on a stereotype of the feudal hierarchy, the palace museum was designed with perfect symmetry. The overall layout demonstrates the supreme authority of the feudal imperial power. An axis is demarcated from south to north, with the three major halls in the front court and the three palaces in the inner court evenly distributed along the axis. The palace museum is arranged with courtyards which are in strict symmetry. Sections are differentiated according to their functions, and the number of rooms is allocated to serve the proper function.

Now the Forbidden City has become the Palace Museum open to the public, together

乾清宫
The Palace of Celestial Purity

with its abundant precious cultural relics and artistic treasures. Halls in the Palaces are now used to exhibit imperial relics. A number of exhibition halls have been set up there, such as the exhibition hall of bronze, the exhibition hall of porcelain, the exhibition hall of Artworks in the Ming and Qing dynasties, the exhibition hall of Art of past dynasties, and the exhibition hall of Jewelry.

▶ 小资料　Data

故宫始建于明永乐四年(1406)，至永乐十八年(1420)基本建成，大体上是在元大都大内的旧址上，以南京宫殿为蓝本设计建造的。这以后又多次续建和重修。

The construction of the Palace Museum started in 1406, the 4th year of Yongle in the Ming Dynasty, It was virtually completed in 1420, the 18th year of Yongle. Based on the layout of palaces in Nanjing, it was built on the old site of the imperial palace of Dadu, the Yuan Dynasty's capital. Hereafter, it was expanded and repaired time and again.

长城

The Great Wall

长城是世界七大奇观之一，是世界上修建时间最长、工程量最大的军事性防御工程，是炎黄子孙血汗与智慧的结晶，也是中华民族坚毅、勤奋的象征。它以宏大的气势和壮美的英姿享誉世界，吸引天下的游人，现已被联合国教科文组织列入世界文化遗产名录。

长城是中国古代用作军事防御的一项宏伟建筑。长城最早大约出现于公元前7—前5世纪。其规模和基础是秦

朝奠定的。以后，汉、南北朝、隋、唐、辽、金、明、清等朝都曾修筑过长城。

八达岭长城

八达岭长城建于明朝，是明朝京城的北大门，在军事上非常重要。它位于北京西北部，依山而筑，城墙高 7.8 米，宽 5.8 米，可以同时让五六匹马并行通过。

居庸关

居庸关在北京的西北部，它修筑在海拔 800 多米的山上，异常险峻。

嘉峪关

嘉峪关在甘肃省境内，是长城最西端的关隘，有"天下雄关"之称。

山海关

山海关位于河北省秦皇岛市境内，有"天下第一关"之称。

1. 八达岭长城
   Badaling Great Wall
2. 金山岭长城
   Jinshanling Great Wall

The Great Wall

The Great Wall, one of the seven wonders in the world, was built to defend against nomadic invaders. It is the largest piece of military defensive engineering in the world which took the longest time to be built, repaired and extended. The Great Wall stands for the crystallization of the blood, sweat and wisdom of Chinese people, a sign of their persistence and diligence as well. The Great Wall is known for its incomparable grandeur, attracting tourists from all over the world. It was inscribed on the world cultual heritage list.

The Great Wall is a remarkable military defensive architecture in ancient China. Its genesis dates back to 700 BC to 500 BC. It was in the Qin Dynasty that the Great Wall really began to take shape. After that, the dynasties

of the Han, South and North, Sui, Tang, Liao, Jin, Ming and Qing successively contributed to the construction of the Great Wall.

The Badaling Great Wall

The Badaling Great Wall was built in the Ming Dynasty. It was a defensive architecture in the north of the capital, playing an important role in terms of military affairs. Lying in the northwest of Beijing, it was built along the mountain ridges. The wall is 7.8 m tall and 5.8 m wide, so it can accommodate five horses abreast.

Juyong Pass

Juyong Pass, situated in the northwest of Beijing, is 800 m above the sea level and is very precipitous and perilous.

Jiayu Pass

Jiayu Pass, located in Gansu Province, is the western terminus of the Great Wall and is reputed to be the most impregnable pass in the world.

Shanhai Pass

Shanhai Pass, situated in the city of Qinhuangdao, Hebei Province, is called "the first pass of the Great Wall".

▶ 你知道吗? *Do you know?*

嘉峪关、居庸关、山海关是万里长城上的三座重要的关隘。

The three major passes of the Great Wall refer to Jiayu Pass, Juyong Pass and Shanhai Pass.

| 2 | 1. 嘉峪关 Jiayu Pass of the Great Wall |
| 1 | 2. 居庸关 Juyong Pass of the Great Wall |

天坛

The Temple of Heaven

天坛是中国现在最大的一处坛庙建筑。原来是明、清两代皇帝祭天、祈祷丰收的地方。位于北京城南永定门内大街东侧。

天坛坛墙有两重，北面呈圆弧形，南面是方直的，象征"天圆地方"。天坛主要建筑有圜丘坛、皇穹宇、祈年殿，还有回音壁、三音石等。

祈年殿原名大祀殿、大享殿，下部为汉白玉砌筑的圆形三层坛体，上面的圆形大殿是鎏金宝顶，覆盖着深蓝色琉璃瓦。圆形大殿象征天空的圆，瓦是蓝色，象征蓝天。殿内支柱的数目，也按照天象设计。

皇穹宇是放置祭天牌位的地方，也是鎏金宝顶、覆盖蓝瓦、尖顶的圆形建筑。它的外面围着圆形的墙，内侧壁面整齐光洁，叫做回音壁，反射声音的效果很明显。

圜丘坛又叫祭天台，每年冬至皇帝在此祭天。祭天台的台阶数目都是九或九的倍数，象征中国神话传说中的九重天。

天坛在中国古代是一个非常神圣的地方，是皇帝和上天沟通交流的地方。现在天坛是全国重点文物保护单位，成为北京的象征之一。

The Temple of Heaven

As the largest alter temple compound in China, the Temple of Heaven was where emperors of the Ming and Qing Dynasties offered sacrifices to heaven and prayed for a good harvest. It is located on the east side of Yongdingmennei Street in the south of Beijing.

The Temple of Heaven is enclosed by two walls. The northern wall is curved while the southern wall is square, standing for the traditional Chinese conception of the round heaven and the square earth. Its main features include the Circular Altar, the Imperial Vault of Heaven, the Hall for the Prayer of Good Harvests, the Echo Wall, the Three Sound Stone, etc.

The Hall for the Prayer of Good Harvests used to be called the Dasi (offering sacrifices to gods or ancestors) Hall and the Daxiang (enjoying sacrifices) Hall. The lower part of the hall is three round terraces made of white marble. The big round hall on the terraces has golden eaves and its roof is covered with dark blue glazed tiles. The round hall stands for the round shape of sky,

and the blue tiles symbolize the blue sky. The number of pillars in the hall was designed according to astronomical observation.

The Imperial Vault of Heaven, which contained tablets of the emperor's ancestors that were used in the solstice ceremony, is also a round architecture with golden eaves, blue tiles and a pointed top. The vault is surrounded by a round wall. The wall's inner side is very smooth and its echo has a marvelous acoustic effect, so the wall is called the Echo Wall.

The Circular Altar is also called the Terrace of Worshiping Heaven. It was where the emperor

offered sacrifice to heaven on the Winter Solstice every year. The number of steps here is 9 or in multiples of the number 9, which signifies the nine layers of heaven in Chinese mythology.

In ancient China the Temple of Heaven was considered a holy place where Emperors communicated with heaven. Now it is a key cultural relic under state protection, and one of the symbols of Beijing.

1 | 2

1. 祈年殿
   The Hall for the Prayer of Good Harvests
2. 回音壁
   The Echo Wall

颐和园

The Summer Palace

颐和园是中国现存最完整的皇家园林，是著名旅游胜地，位于北京城西北郊，主要由万寿山和昆明湖组成。

颐和园内有山有水，整体构思巧妙，是世界上罕见的园林杰作。佛香阁是颐和园的标志，是中国古建筑中的精品。长廊以其梁枋上绘有 8 000 多幅变化无穷的山水、人物、花鸟画而久负盛名。德和园大戏楼为清代三大戏台之一。谐趣园是园中之园，具有江南园林特色。

The Summer Palace

The Summer Palace is the most intact imperial garden that has been preserved in China. It is a famous scenic spot located in the northwest suburbs of Beijing. It is mainly made up of the Kunming Lake and Longevity Hill.

The Summer Palace integrates mountains and water into an ingenious whole. It is a rare masterpiece of garden design in the world. The Buddhist Incense Tower is the symbol of the vast Summer Palace compound, and a fine work of art in Chinese ancient architecture, too. The Long Corridor is famous for its shaded walkway that is decorated with some 8 000 painted scenes of mountains, water, people, flowers and birds. The private theater in the Hall for Cultivating Happiness is one of the three big theaters in the Qing Dynasty. The Garden of Harmonious Delights is the best of all gardens in the Summer Palace, with the characteristics of Jiangnan (area south of the lower reaches of the Yangtze River) gardens.

 小资料 Data

现在颐和园的前身是清漪园。清乾隆十五年 (1750)，乾隆为了庆祝母亲 60 岁生日，开始对它进行修整。英法联军入侵北京后，西郊园林被焚毁。慈禧太后动用海军经费修复了万寿山清漪园。光绪十四年 (1887) 更名为 "颐和园"，表达的是 "颐养冲和" 的意思。颐和园后来再次遭到八国联军洗劫，两年后重修。

The Summer Palace didn't take on its present appearance until Emperor Qianlong of the Qing Dynasty reconstructed it into the Garden of Clear Ripples for his mother's 60th birthday in 1750, the 15th year of his reign. During the Second Opium War, gardens in the western suburbs including the Summer Palace were looted and partially destroyed by French and British forces. After that, Empress Dowager Cixi diverted funds earmarked to build a modern Chinese navy and spent the money to repair the Longevity Hill and Garden of Clear Ripples. In 1887, the 14th year during Emperor Guangxu's reign, she gave the palace its current name, *yiheyuan*, which means the "Garden for Cultivating Harmony". Later, Western armies sacked the Summer Palace again. Two years later, it was rebuilt.

1	
2	3

1. 昆明湖和万寿山
   The Kunming Lake and Longevity Hill
2. 佛香阁
   The Buddhist Incense Tower
3. 长廊
   The Long Corridor

承德避暑 山庄

Chengde Imperial Summer Villa

承德避暑山庄是中国现存最大的古代皇家园林，在河北省承德市武列河西岸，面积564万平方米，是中国重点文物保护单位和重点风景名胜区。

避暑山庄是清初的康熙皇帝为了巩固北部边防，处理边疆民族政务而兴建的一所宫廷性质的园林，除了供夏季居住游赏，还具有着特殊的纪念意义。

园内模拟了很多国内的重要景观。东南方的湖泊，模拟江南水乡；北面的草地，模拟北方蒙古草原；西部的山峦，模拟高原山区；山上的城墙式宫墙，模拟万里长城。

承德外八庙

承德外八庙是中国河北承德避暑山庄外的喇嘛寺院群，一共11座，因其中8座被8处办事机构管理，所以叫外八庙，现仅存7座。它们绝大多数是为了来热河行宫朝见清帝的蒙藏王公贵族观瞻、居住而建造的，是一批政治性很强的纪念性建筑。

11座庙宇按照建筑风格分为藏式寺庙、汉式寺庙和汉藏结合式寺庙三种。这些寺庙融合了汉、藏等民族建筑艺术的精华，气势宏伟，具有皇家风范。这11座建筑风格各异的寺庙，是当时清政府为了团结蒙古、新疆、西藏等地区的少数民族而修建的，雄伟壮观。

Chengde
Imperial Summer Villa

Chengde Imperial Summer Villa is the largest extant ancient imperial garden compound in China. Located on the west bank of the Wulie River in Chengde City of Hebei Province, it has an area of 5 640 000 m². It is a key cultural relic under state protection and an important scenic spot.

The Imperial Summer Villa was built during the reign of Emperor Kangxi of the early Qing Dynasty to consolidate frontier defense and deal with the affairs of ethnic minorities in border areas. It is a garden with the characteristics of an imperial palace. It is not only a summer retreat but also a place with special commemorative significance.

A number of major scenes in China are replicated in this Imperial Summer Villa. The lakes in the southeast model themselves on lakes in Jiangnan, the grassland in the north is a duplication of Mongolian grasslands in northern China, the mountains in the west resemble plateaus and mountainous areas, and the palace wall on the mountains imitates the Great Wall.

The Eight Outer Temples of Chengde

The Eight Outer Temples of Chengde are clusters of Lamaist temples around the Imperial Summer Villa. There are altogether 11 temples. Eight of them used to be administrated by eight organizations — hence the name "Eight Outer Temples". Now there are only seven left. The majority of them were built to accommodate Mongolian and Tibetan nobility who went to visit the Qing emperors. The temples have strong political and commemorative significance.

In terms of architectural style, the 11 temples can be classified into three types — Tibetan-style, Han-style and Han-Tibetan blending style. These temples embody the essence of the architectural arts of various nationalities like Han and Tibet. Grandiose and imperially imposing, the 11 temples with distinct styles were built by the Qing government to promote unity with ethnic minorities in the regions of Mongolia, Xinjiang and Tibet.

▶ 小资料 Data

承德避暑山庄历史上叫做热河行宫，一般称承德离宫，始建于康熙四十二年 (1703)，建成于乾隆五十五年 (1790)。

The Chengde Imperial Summer Villa was called Rehe Xanadu in history, conventionally known as *Chengde Ligong* (a temporary abode for an emperor on progresses). Its construction began in the 42nd year (1703) of Emperor Kangxi's reign and was completed in the 55th year (1790) of Emperor Qianlong's reign.

1. 上帝阁
   Shangdi Tower
2. 承德外八庙
   The Eight Outer Temples of Chengde

明十三陵

The Ming Tombs

明十三陵是明代帝王的陵墓群，在北京市西北郊昌平区境内。陵区是一个小盆地，北、东、西三面有许多山，南面龙、虎二山分别在左右，符合中国古代帝王选择陵墓的风水思想。从 1409 年开始，先后修建了一共十三座陵寝，所以叫十三陵。这里共埋葬了 13 位皇帝、23 位皇后和众多嫔妃、太子、公主以及从葬宫女等。

明十三陵中，天寿山中峰下的长陵最宏伟。工程精细的是大峪山下的定陵。1956 年发掘了定陵地宫。地宫出土珍贵文物近 3 000 件，其中有许多精美工艺品。

陵区东南有十三陵水库，水库南面建有北京九龙游乐园。陵区松柏葱郁，果树成林，景色美丽，是旅游胜地。

The Ming Tombs

The tombs of 13 emperors of the Ming Dynasty are scattered in a small basin in the Changping County on the northwest outskirts of Beijing. They are surrounded by hills on the north, east and west sides. The Dragon Hill and the Tiger Hill guard the tombs on the left and right sides, which conform to *fengshui* that would always influence ancient emperors in choosing their tombs. From 1409 on, 13 tombs were built there, hence the name Shisanling(13 tombs). Here are buried 13 emperors, 23 empresses, many concubines of the emperors, crown princes, princesses and maids of honor.

Of the 13 tombs, the Changling Tomb at the foot of the central peak of the Tianshou Hill is the grandest, and the Dingling Tomb at the bottom of the Dayu Hill is the most exquisitely built. Excavation of the Dingling Tomb occurred in 1956 and about 3 000 precious artifacts were found in the underground tomb, many of which are refined works of art.

Southeast of the tombs is the Ming Tombs Reservoir, and the Nine-dragon Entertainment Park is to the south of the reservoir. With its beautiful scenery of verdant pines and cypresses and groves of fruit trees, the Ming Tombs scenic area is an ideal tourist resort.

1 | 2

1. 俯瞰十三陵
   A bird's-eye view of the Ming Tombs
2. 定陵地宫
   The Dingling Tomb

秦始皇陵与秦始皇兵马俑博物馆

The Qinshihuang Mausoleum and the
Museum of the Terracotta Warriors and Horses

秦始皇陵与秦始皇兵马俑博物馆在陕西省临潼县境内，是目前世界上最大的帝王陵墓博物馆，号称"世界第八奇观"，现已被联合国教科文组织列入世界文化遗产名录。

秦始皇陵是秦始皇13岁即位后，动用70多万人，花了36年的时间建成的。陵墓长515米，宽485米，高76米，就像金字塔一样。

在秦始皇陵东侧1 500米的地方有三个举世闻名的兵马俑坑。数量巨大、造型精美的陶塑兵马俑布置成军阵场面，面向东方、气势磅礴、威武雄壮，再现了秦始皇军队的力量和气派，具有强大的艺术感染力，表现出中国历史上第一个皇帝秦始皇的"示强威、服海内"的王者霸气。这也是秦朝宫廷禁卫军的真实表现，象征着守卫陵园的职能。

The **Qinshihuang**
Mausoleum and the Museum of the Terracotta Warriors and Horses

The Qinshihuang Mausoleum and the Museum of Terracotta Warriors and Horses, situated in Lintong County of Shaanxi Province, is the largest imperial mausoleum museum in the world. Known as "the eighth wonder in the world", UNESCO listed them as one of the world's cultural heritage sites.

The project of building the Qinshihuang Mausoleum began when Qinshihuang ascended to the throne at the age of 13. It took over 700 000 laborers over 36 years to finish the pyramid like building, which is 515 m long, 485 m wide and 76 m high.

Somewhere 1 500 m to the east of the Qinshihuang Mausoleum are three world-famous pits containing terracotta warriors and horses. Displayed in them are thousands of exquisite terracotta warriors and horses forming battle arrays. The life-size warriors and horses face the east, standing in an imposing manner. They demonstrate the dominant power and dignified air of Qinshihuang's troops with a strong artistic appeal. They also epitomize the powerful leadership of Qinshihuang, the first emperor in Chinese history. This is also the representation of the Imperial Guard in the Qin Dynasty who would protect the whole mausoleum.

▶ 小资料　Data

秦俑坑修建工程约始于公元前 221 年秦朝统一六国之后，到公元前 209 年因陈胜、吴广起义被迫停工。应该是秦始皇在世的时候，从全国各地征调大批工匠、罪犯来服徭役制作的。

The construction of the terracotta warriors and horses pits began in 221 BC when the Qin Dynasty unified China by merging the other 6 states, and was forced to stop in 209 BC because of the uprising led by Chen Sheng and Wu Guang. The project was carried out by craftsmen and culprits conscripted from all over the country when Qinshihuang was still alive.

1 | 2

1. 一号兵马俑坑
   The No.1 Pit of Terracotta Warriors and Horses of the Mausoleum of Emperor Qinshihuang
2. 将军俑
   Terracotta General

敦煌莫高窟

The Mogao Grottoes in Dunhuang

　　莫高窟又叫"千佛洞"，位于甘肃省敦煌东南 25 千米的鸣沙山东麓，是中国四大石窟之一，也是世界上最大、内容最多的佛教石窟群，现已被联合国教科文组织列入世界文化遗产名录。

　　莫高窟始建于 366 年，南北长 1 610 米。现有洞窟 492 个，壁画 45 000 多平方米，彩塑 2 000 多尊。

　　石窟大小不等，塑像高矮不一，大的雄伟浑厚，小的精巧玲珑。壁画精美绝伦，内容多为佛经故事。艺术造诣精深，想象力丰富，令人惊叹。

　　敦煌石窟艺术中数量最大、内容最丰富的部分是壁画。这些壁画具有很高的历史和艺术价值，其中盛唐时期的壁画水平最高。西方学者将敦煌壁画称作是"墙壁上的图书馆"。

The Mogao Grottoes in Dunhuang

The Mogao Grottoes, also called the "Cave of Ten Thousand Buddhas", are located on the eastern foot of the Mingsha (singing sand) Mountain 25 km southeast of Dunhuang in Gansu Province. They are one of the four great grottoes in China and also the largest Buddhist grottoes with the most substantive contents in the world. Now they have been listed as one of world cultural heritage sites.

The Mogao Grottoes, originally built in 366 AD, extend 1 610 m from south to north. There are 492 caves and 45 000 m² of murals and over 2 000 statues in different colors.

The caves are different in size and the statues are varied in height. The big statues are grand and the small ones are refined. The murals are extremely exquisite and mainly depict the stories of Buddhist scriptures. Their high artistic attainment and the rich imagination impress visitors with breathless admiration.

Of all the art forms of the Dunhuang Grottoes, murals have the largest number and the richest content. These murals are of great historical and artistic value. The murals painted in the prime of the Tang Dynasty are of the highest attainment. No wonder some scholars in the west call the Dunhuang Grottoes "the library on walls".

▶ 小资料 Data

洞窟中除了壁画和彩塑外，还有大量经卷、文书，这为研究中国古代的政治、经济、军事、文化、艺术、宗教、民族史等提供了宝贵的资料。

如果把莫高窟的壁画连接起来，可长达30千米。壁画不仅体现了中国的民族风格，而且吸取了印度、罗马、埃及等国古代艺术之长，是东西方文化的结晶。

Apart from murals and colorful statues, there are a large number of scriptures and documents that provide precious information for the research of politics, economics, military affairs, culture, arts, religion and the national history of ancient China.

If one joins all the murals of the Mogao Grottoes together, they may stretch for 30 km. The murals not only represent the national style of China but also absorb the advantages from the ancient arts of India, Rome, Egypt, etc. It is merging quintessence of both East and West cultures.

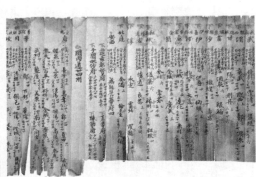

$\frac{1}{2}$ | 3

1. 彩塑菩萨像
   Colorful Buddha statue
2. 莫高窟外观
   The Mogao Grottoes
3. 藏经洞内的经书
   Buddhist scriptures in the cave

丽江古城

The Old Town of Lijiang

丽江古城位于云南省西北部，距今已有800多年的历史。

古城街道自由分布，主街傍水，小巷临渠，76座古石桥与河水、绿树、古巷、古屋相依相映，被誉为"东方威尼斯"和"高原姑苏"。

古城心脏四方街在明清时已是滇西北商贸枢纽，是茶马古道上的集散中心。古城中至今依然大片保持明清建筑特色，被中外建筑专家誉为"民居博物馆"。

丽江古城文物古迹众多，文化底蕴丰厚独特，是我国保存最完整、最具民族风格的古代城镇。"东巴文化"中的"东巴文"和"纳西古乐"是世界文化史上的奇葩，是活化石。1997年12月4日，丽江被联合国教科文组织正式批准列入世界文化遗产名录。

玉龙雪山

玉龙雪山位于丽江县城北面约13千米处。山势由北向南走向，雪山面积960平方千米，高山雪域风景位于海拔4 500米以上。

The Old Town of **Lijiang**

Perched in the northwest of Yunnan Province, the Old Town of Lijiang has a history of over 800 years.

The Old Town's streets are distributed freely. The main streets are close to rivers and small lanes are near cannels. The town is decorated with over 76 stone bridges, crisscrossing rivers flowing with water, verdant trees, ancient lanes, and old houses. This harmonious scene earns Lijiang the reputation of "Oriental Venice" and "Gusu on the Plateau".

At the heart of the old town is the Square Street. Centuries ago in the Ming and Qing Dynasties, it was the central bazaar in the northwest of Yunnan Province, and the crossroads for trade in the Tea-Horse Ancient Road (an important transportation line for the southwest of ancient China). Lijiang has preserved many old buildings with the Ming and Qing styles. That is why it is called by architecture experts at home and abroad "the Museum of Dwelling Houses".

The Old Town of Lijiang has myriads of historical relics and rich culture. It is an ancient town that has been best preserved and has the most distinctive ethnic styles in China. The "Dongba character" of "Dongba culture" and the "Naxi ancient music" are just like the living fossils in the Chinese culture history. On Dec.4, 1997, Lijiang was added to the world cultual heritage list.

Jade Dragon Snow Mountain
Jade Dragon Snow Mountain is 13 km away from the north of Lijiang, running from the north to the south with a coverage area of 960 km^2. The high-mountain snow scenery stands at above 4 500 m in altitude.

1|2| 3

1. 古城风貌
   The Old Town of Lijiang
2. 四方街
   The Square Street
3. 玉龙雪山
   Jade Dragon Snow Mountain

平遥 古城

The Ancient City of Pingyao

　　平遥古城城墙始建于周宣王时期，现在保存的平遥城墙是中国明代重筑扩建的，在山西省平遥县。

　　平遥城墙马面多，分段筑，一共有 71 堵，造型美观，防御设施齐备。古城的筑城手法古老，工程实施和材料选用都十分精良，是研究中国古代筑城的珍贵资料。

　　平遥城池呈方形，城墙周长 6 163 米。平遥城墙共有 3 000 个垛口，加上 72 座敌楼，据说象征着"孔子七十二贤人，三千弟子"。这里古老的城内建筑与城墙相互衬托，古城风貌依然可见。平遥古城不仅是国家历史文化名城，还被联合国教科文组织列入了世界文化遗产名录。

The Ancient City of **Pingyao**

The ancient city walls of Pingyao County in Shanxi Province were originally erected during the reign of Emperor Xuan of the Zhou Dynasty, and the extant walls were rebuilt and extended during the Ming Dynasty.

Pingyao has 71 walls, which were built separately with many *mamian* (the protruding flat). The walls are not only pleasing to the eye but also complete with all the defensive facilities. The methods of the city's construction were old in fashion, and the process of construction and the choice of materials were careful. The city walls serve as a precious historic record of China's ancient wall construction.

The ancient city of Pingyao sprawls in a square shape, with a perimeter of 6 163 m. There are 72 watchtowers and 3 000 crenels on the city walls — symbolizing the 72 virtuous students of Confucius and his 3 000 disciples respectively. Here old buildings and walls enhance each other's beauty and make people feel that the past is alive in Pingyao. Pingyao is not only a famous historic and cultural city in the country, but also a name inscribed on the world cultural heritage list by UNESCO.

1 | 2

1. 平遥古城
   The Ancient City of Pingyao
2. 平遥街景
   A glimpse of the street in Pingyao

皖南 古村落

Ancient Villages in Southern Anhui

皖南古村落是指安徽省境内长江以南地区在清末以前形成的具有历史、艺术、科学价值的民居、祠堂、书院、牌坊及楼台亭阁等建筑群，具有强烈的徽州文化特色。西递、宏村古民居是安徽南部民居中最具有代表性的两座古村落。2000 年 11 月，西递、宏村同时被联合国教科文组织列入世界文化遗产名录。

宏村

宏村，位于安徽省黄山市黟县。由于这里地势较高，经常云蒸霞蔚，有时如浓墨重彩，有时似泼墨写意，好似一幅山水长卷，因此被誉为"中国画里的乡村"。

古宏村人开"仿生学"先河，规划并建造了牛形村落和人工水系，成为当今"建筑史上一大奇观"。这种设计堪称"中华一绝"。

全村现有完好保存的明清民居140余幢。著名景点有承志堂、南湖书院等。

承志堂

承志堂被誉为"民间故宫"，由清代盐商营造，占地2000多平方米，为砖木结构楼房。此房气势恢宏，工艺精细。其正厅横梁、斗拱、花门、窗棂上的木刻层次繁复，人物众多，被誉为"徽派木雕工艺陈列馆"。

西 递

西递坐落于黄山南麓黟县境内。整个村落呈船形，现有居民300余户，保存有完整的古民居122幢，被誉为"中国传统文化的缩影"和"中国明清民居博物馆"。

这里所有街巷均以黟县青石铺地，古建筑多为木结构，由砖墙维护，建筑上的木雕、石雕、砖雕丰富多彩，是中国徽派建筑艺术的典型代表。目前已开发的有凌云阁、大夫第等20余处景点。

大夫第

"大夫第"为临街亭阁式建筑，原用于观景，楼额悬有"桃花源里人家"六个大字。有趣的是，近人多将此楼当作古装戏中小姐择婿"热抛绣球"所在，现已成为西递村举办此项民俗活动的场所。

1 | 2

1. 宏村
   The Hongcun Village
2. 宏村承志堂
   The Chengzhi Hall, Hongcun Village

Ancient Villages in **Southern Anhui**

Located in the south area of the Yangtze River in Anhui Province, ancient villages in southern Anhui have private homes, ancestral temples, academies, memorial archways, pagodas, verandas, etc. that were built before the end of the Qing Dynasty and are of great value in the research fields of history, art and science. The architecture there has strong Huizhou (another name for Anhui) characteristics. Xidi and Hongcun are the most typical of the ancient villages of southern Anhui, and both of them were simultaneously added to the world cultural heritage list by UNESCO in November, 2000.

The Hongcun Village

The Hongcun village is located in Yixian County, Huangshan City, Anhui Province. Since it is comparatively high in elevation, it is always bathed in colorful clouds and rays of sunshine. It looks very much like a roll of landscape painting — alternatively looming between heavy color, and bold splash-inked (a technique of Chinese ink-painting) outline. So it is praised as "the village in a traditional Chinese painting".

Ancient residents of Hongcun were pioneers of bionics. They were the first to have planned and built the cow-shaped village and artificial river system. This design is thought to be a wonder in the architectural history and a miracle in China.

Now there are over 140 Ming and Qing dwelling houses that have been well preserved in the village. The famous scenic spots are the Chengzhi Hall, Nanhu Academy and so on.

The Chengzhi Hall

The Chengzhi Hall has the reputation of "the Palace Museum of folk style". It is a brick-wood building first built by a salt merchant in the Qing Dynasty, with an area of over 2 000 m^2. Exquisitely built, it stands in all its imposing glory. There are complicated wood carvings depicting many characters on the crossbeams of the main hall, on the top of the columns, on flower-carven doors and on the window frames. So the Chengzhi Hall is also called "the museum of wood carvings of Anhui style".

The Xidi Village

The Xidi village is located in Yixian County, Huangshan City, Anhui Province. The whole village looks very similar to a boat. In the village of over 300 families, there are 122 ancient dwelling houses kept intact. It is called "the epitome of Chinese traditional culture", and "China's museum of dwelling houses of the Ming and Qing Dynasties".

All the streets and lanes here are paved with stone slabs produced in Yixian Country. The old buildings are mainly built by wooden structure, maintained by brick walls. Carvings on wood, marble and brick of the buildings vary in shape and color, presenting a typical Anhui style. There are over 20 scenic spots open to public, such as the Lingyun Tower and the Dafudi Pavilion.

The Dafudi Pavilion

The Dafudi Pavilion is a pavilion overlooking the street. It was built for a better view of local scenery. On the pavilion hangs a horizontal inscribed board with the six characters "Tao Hua Yuan Li Ren Jia (people living in the Land of Peach Blossoms — a fictitious land of peace away from the turmoil of the world)". People usually think that the Dafudi Pavilion is the place where a young unmarried lady chooses her husband by throwing a ball made of rolled colored silk, as is shown in some ancient costume in today's TV plays. Now it has become a venue for carrying out this type of folk activity in the Xidi Village.

1. 宏村桃园居厢房木雕
   Wood carving in the Hongcun Village
2. 西递大夫第 "绣楼"
   The Pavilion for young ladies of the Dafudi, Xidi Village

杭州 西湖

The West Lake

西湖位于浙江省杭州市区西面，是著名的旅游胜地。

苏堤与白堤把全湖分为外湖、里湖、岳湖、西里湖和小南湖5个部分。湖中有三岛：三潭印月、湖心亭、阮公墩。人们常常把杭州西湖和瑞士日内瓦的莱蒙湖比喻为世界上东西辉映的两颗明珠，正是因为有了西湖，马可·波罗赞誉杭州为"世界上最美丽华贵的天城"。

"西湖"一名始于唐朝。宋朝苏东坡咏诗赞美西湖说："水光潋滟晴方好，山色空蒙雨亦奇。欲把西湖比西子，淡妆浓抹总相宜。"诗人别出心裁地把西湖比作我国古代传说中的美人西施，于是西湖又多了一个"西子湖"的雅号。

西湖风光秀丽，景色迷人。西湖之美，美在一年四季，美在一日四时，美在阴、晴、雨、雪、雾中。

The West Lake

The West Lake is located in the west of Hangzhou City, Zhejiang Province. It is a famous scenic spot.

be pearls in the world, shining from the occident and orient and enhancing each other's beauty. Thanks to the West Lake,

always alluring." In his poem, Su uniquely compared the West Lake to Xizi, a legendary beautiful woman in ancient

The Su Causeway and Bai Causeway divide the whole lake into five distinct sections — the Outer Lake, the Inner Lake, the Yuehu Lake, the West Inner Lake and the Small South Lake. Three isles are in the lake and they are called "Three Pools Mirroring the Moon", "Pavilions in the Middle of the Lake" and "Ruan Gong Isle". The West Lake of Hangzhou enjoys the equal fame with Lac Léman (or Lake Geneva) in Geneva, Switzerland, both reputed to

Hangzhou has become "the most beautiful and luxurious city in the world", according to ancient Italian tourist Marco Polo.

The name of "West Lake" was first used in the Tang Dynasty. In the Song Dynasty, a famous poet called Su Dongpo wrote the following stanzas to glorify this beautiful lake, "Rippling water shimmering on sunny day, misty mountains shrouded the rain; Plain or gaily decked out like Xizi, West Lake is

China, and hence the elegant name "Xizi Lake".

The beauty of the West Lake lies in its lingering charm that survives the change of seasons in a year, of hours in a day, and of different weathers, no matter if it is cloudy, sunny, rainy, snowy, or foggy.

1 | 2 1. 西湖
       The West Lake
    2. 三潭印月
       Three Pools Mirroring the Moon

桂林 山水

The Scenery of Guilin

桂林山水以桂林市为中心，北起兴安灵渠，南至阳朔，由漓江一水相连，集"山清、水秀、洞奇、石美"四绝于一体，有"桂林山水甲天下"的美称。

独秀峰

独秀峰是桂林十大景观之一。要爬上山峰的顶端，必须经过306级蜿蜒的石阶。山崖上，有历代文人题写的摩崖石刻，具有一定的历史和艺术价值。

象鼻山

象鼻山在漓江西岸，它的形状就像一头巨象站在江边伸长鼻子喝水，形象逼真。

七星岩

七星岩在漓江东岸，是桂林最著名的溶洞，分上、中、下三层。洞内有地下河、地下画廊，以及许多石钟乳、石笋、石柱等。

漓江

桂林漓江风景区是中国最著名的岩溶山水风景区。这里奇峰对峙，飞瀑连连，峰峦叠秀，碧水如镜，景色无比秀美。

The Scenery of **Guilin**

1 | 2

1. 阳朔风光
   A splendid view of Yangshuo
2. 漓江渔火
   A fishing boat along the Lijiang River

▶ 小知识 Knowledge

桂林山水位于石灰岩分布地区，这里山多、洞多、水也多，有"无山不洞、无洞不奇"的赞句。

The landscape in Guilin is located in an area where limestone is extensively distributed. There are myriads of mountains, caves and waterways, as the saying goes "there is no mountain without caves and there is no cave without unique scenery in Guilin".

The unique scenery of Guilin, with Guilin City in the center and the Lijiang River as its backdrop, ranges from Lingqu of Xing'an in the north and to Yangshuo in the south. It prominently features verdant mountains, limpid waters, special caves and beautiful rocks. "Guilin's scenery is the most beautiful in China," so goes a Chinese saying.

Duxiu Peak

Duxiu Peak is one of the ten major attractions in Guilin, with the winding 306 stone steps leading to the summit of the peak. On the cliff there are inscriptions of poems by the literati of past dynasties, which are of certain historical and artistic value.

Elephant Trunk Hill

Elephant Trunk Hill, on the west bank of the Lijiang River, looks vividly like an elephant dipping its trunk into the river to drink water.

The Seven-Star Cave

The Seven-Star Cave, on the east bank of the Lijiang River, is the most famous cave in Guilin. It falls into upper, middle and lower levels. Underground rivers, underground galleries and many stalactites, stalagmites and stone pillars, etc. can be found in the cave.

The Lijiang River

The Lijiang River scenic area of Guilin is the most famous karst scenic spot in China. There are grotesque peaks standing facing each other, along with flying waterfalls, hills rising one upon another and water as clear as a mirror. In a word, the scenery is incomparably attractive.

武陵源

Wulingyuan

武陵源位于中国湖南省西北部张家界市的武陵源区，由张家界、天子山、索溪峪三大风景区组成，方圆369平方千米。这里有原始生态体系的砂岩、峰林、峡谷地貌，奇峰众多，姿态万千。

与自然风光相呼应的是武陵源纯朴的田园风光。这里有土家族、苗族等少数民族的聚居地，梯田、房舍星星点点，点缀在青山绿水间。在当地的少数民族节日里，人们载歌载舞。这一切与武陵源的风光浑然一体，构成一幅美丽的画卷。

张家界

张家界是中国第一个国家级森林公园。这里森林资源极其丰富，植物种类繁多。景点有60多处，主要有金鞭溪、袁家界等。

索溪峪风景区

索溪峪风景区是武陵源风景区的中心和门户，风景独特，主要由十里画廊、宝峰湖及黄龙洞三个景区组成。

天子山风景区

天子山风景区峰林如海，气象万千，是观赏砂岩峰林的绝佳之处，以御笔峰、云青岩、神堂湾及大观台为最佳观景台。

Wulingyuan

The Wulingyuan Scenic Spot, situated in the Wulingyuan District of Zhangjiajie City in the northwest of Hunan Province, includes the Zhangjiajie National Forest Park, the Suoxiyu Natural Reserve and the Tianzi Mountain Natural Reserve. Covering an area of 369 km², Wulingyuan boasts its sandstones, forests of peaks and canyons in their primitive ecological state. There are also numerous peculiar peaks in their distinctive postures.

Apart from its natural beauty, Wulingyuan also has peaceful rustic scenery. It is the home of several China's minority groups, such as Tujia, Miao, etc. The green mountains and water here are dotted with terraces and houses. People dance and sing during the minority groups' festivals. All of the idyllic scenery blends with Wulingyuan's amazing landscape into a beautiful integrated picture.

Zhangjiajie

Zhangjiajie is the first national forest park in China. It has rich forest resources and numerous species of plants. There are over 60 scenic attractions, such as the Golden Whip Stream, Yuanjiajie, etc.

The Suoxiyu Scenic Spot

The Suoxiyu Scenic Spot is the center and gateway of Wulingyuan. The three biggest attractions include the Ten Li Corridor, the Baofeng Lake and the Yellow Dragon Cave.

The Tianzi Mountain Scenic Spot

The Tianzi Mountain Scenic Spot has a sea of peaks and thousands of different scenes. It is an ideal place to observe sandstone peaks. The Imperial Brush Peak, the Cloud Blue Rock, the Divine Hall Bay and the Grand View Terrace are the places that offer the best view.

1 | 2
1. 张家界
   Zhangjiajie
2. 索溪峪
   Suoxiyu

黄龙 风景区

Huanglong

黄龙风景名胜区位于四川省阿坝藏族羌族自治州，海拔在3 000米以上，是中国最高的风景名胜区之一。

黄龙风景名胜区岩溶景观独特，动植物资源非常丰富，人文景观也相当吸引人。相传很久以前曾有"黄龙真人"在这里隐居修道。现在每逢农历六月中黄龙寺传统庙会，附近的藏、羌、回、汉各族群众会来这里聚会，入寺祈祷，游乐赏景，载歌载舞。

▶ **小资料** Knowledge

地表钙华是黄龙景观的最大特色，它们集中在一条沟（即黄龙沟）中。黄龙沟地表的钙华形成钙华堤，并造成大片"五彩池"。在沟中还有一个长达2 500米的钙华滩，造成"金沙铺地"奇观，使整个沟谷金光闪闪，很像一条巨大的黄龙从雪山上飞腾而下，黄龙沟因此得名。

Colored travertine ponds are the main landscape in Huanglong. They are concentrated mainly in a ditch called Huanglonggou Ditch. The calcium carbonate in the ponds deposited to form travertine dykes and a large area of so-called "five-colored ponds". In the ditch there is a travertine shoal about 2 500 m long. This marvelous spectacle of golden sand covering the ground makes the whole ditch glimmer with golden rays. The scene looks like a gigantic yellow dragon rushing down the snow mountain. Hence, the ditch wins the name of "Huanglong (yellow dragon) Ditch".

1	2
	3

1. 黄龙风景区
   The Huanglong Scenic Spot
2. 金沙铺地
   The ground of golden sand
3. 黄龙五彩池
   Five-colored ponds in Huanglong

Huanglong

Huanglong is located in the Aba Tibet and Qiang Autonomous Prefecture in the northwest of Sichuan Province. With an altitude of over 3 000 m, it is one of the highest scenic areas in China.

This area is known for its unique colorful pools formed by calcite deposits. It has abundant plant and animal resources and also attractive human activities. According to the legend, there was a sage called "Huanglong Zhenren" who withdrew from the earthy world to live here in solitude and practiced Taoism. In the middle of the sixth lunar month every year, a traditional temple fair at Huanglong usually attracts a large number of local people of Tibet, Qiang, Hui and Han Nationalities. The fairgoers assemble here to pray in the temple, enjoy the scenery, festively singing and dancing.

九寨沟

Jiuzhaigou (The Nine-Village Valley)

的湖泊，飞瀑、溪流把它们连接在一起，沟尾有诺日朗瀑布。日则沟的珍珠滩瀑布是九寨沟最奇特的瀑布。

景区在 20 世纪 70 年代被发现，1992 年被联合国教科文组织纳入世界自然文化遗产名录，1997 年被纳入世界"人与生物圈"保护网络，是迄今为止世界上唯一同时获得这两项殊荣的景区。

▶ 你知道吗？ Do you know?

九寨沟景观的奇特之处，首先在于它有 108 个"翠海"（当地人习惯称湖泊为"海子"）。传说在很久以前，神女沃诺色姆的情人达戈送给她一面宝镜，她可能是太高兴了，不小心把宝镜摔成了 108 块，碎片变成了彩色湖泊"翠海"。

The unique charm of Jiuzhaigou scenery lies in its 108 jade seas (local people call lakes haizi, meaning"sea"in Chinese). Legend has it that the goddess Wonosmo got a mystical mirror, a gift of love from the god Dag. Being overjoyed, she dropped the mirror and the broken pieces became the 108"jade seas".

九寨沟风景名胜区位于四川省阿坝藏族羌族自治州，是一条纵深 50 多千米的山沟谷地，因为沟内有 9 个藏族村寨而得名。

沟中有湖泊、瀑布、雪山、森林，景物特异，原始自然，被称为"童话世界"。长海、剑岩、诺日朗、树正、扎如、黑海六大景区以翠海、叠瀑、彩林、雪峰、藏情而驰名中外。

树正景区很有特点，总长 50 多千米的主沟内有 108 个奇特

Jiuzhaigou (The Nine-Village Valley)

Set in Aba Tibet and Qiang Autonomous Prefecture of Sichuan Province, Jiuzhaigou is a valley more than 50 km long. The name Jiuzhaigou comes from the nine Tibetan villages scattered along the valley.

The scenery in Jiuzhaigou impresses people with its colorful ponds, waterfalls, snow-capped mountains, and forests. Its peculiar and primitive sights earn it the name "fairy land". The famous six scenic spots there include the Long Lake, Sword Rock, Nuorilang, Shuzheng, Zharu Valley and Black Lake. They are world-famous for the emerald green lakes, rushing cascades, colorful forests, snow peaks and Tibetan customs.

The Shuzheng scenic area has its special characteristics. The 50-km-long valley is decorated with 108 exotic lakes which are connected by waterfalls and streams. The Nuorilang Waterfall is located at the end of the valley. The Waterfall of Pearl Shoal in Rizegou is the most exotic waterfall in Jiuzhaigou.

Discovered in the 1970s, Jiuzhaigou was inscribed on the world natural heritage list in 1992, and was added to the protection network of the world's "Man and Biosphere". It is the only place in the world that enjoys both of the two honors.

1 | 2
| 3
| 4

1. 珍珠滩瀑布
   The Waterfall of Pearl Shoal
2. 熊猫海
   The Panda Sea
3. 犀牛海
   The Rhinoceros sea
4. 九寨沟五彩池
   Five-colored ponds in Jiuzhaigou

布达拉宫

The Potala Palace

布达拉宫位于西藏拉萨古城之西的布达拉山上，是中国喇嘛教首领达赖喇嘛居住的地方，也是清朝时候西藏政、教合一的统治中心。

布达拉宫全部建筑面积在10万平方米以上。宫殿主体建筑都是包山头而建造，连同山基高达117米，好像破山而出，直插向高原的蓝天，具有非凡的艺术感染力。

宫殿位于西藏拉萨郊区的河谷地带，建筑包括宫城区、宫室区及后山湖区。宫城内是为布达拉宫服务的管理机关、印经院、僧俗官员的住宅、监狱、马厩等。山顶的宫室区是以白宫和红宫为主体的大建筑群。白宫专为达赖喇嘛政治和宗教生活服务，达赖喇嘛的宫室在白宫大殿堂的顶层；红宫是宗教性建筑群，由已故达赖喇嘛的灵塔殿和其他一些殿堂组成。在白宫和红宫的南面，是供僧人进行宗教活动的经堂。

▶ **小资料 Data**

> 布达拉宫始建于公元7世纪。在清朝顺治二年(1645年)五世达赖时期大加扩建，经过历代达赖喇嘛的扩建，才形成现在所看到的规模。
>
> The Potala Palace was originally built in the 7th century. In 1645, the 2nd year of Shunzhi reign of the Qing Dynasty, the 5th Dalai Lama expanded the construction. And it came to the present size after successive expansions.

The Potala Palace

Situated on the Potala Mountain west of the ancient city of Lhasa in Tibet, the Potala Palace is the residential place of the Dalai Lama, the head of Tibetan Buddhism. It was also the political and religious center of Tibet in the Qing Dynasty.

The Potala Palace has a floor space of more than 100 000 m². The main part of the palace is constructed on the mountain. Together with the mountain base, it is 117 m high. It seems that the palace pops up from the mountain, stabbing into the blue sky on the plateau. This scene has an extraordinary artistic appeal.

The Potala Palace is located in the valley in the suburbs of Lhasa in Tibet. The architectural complex is divided into the Palace-City area, the Palace-Room area and the lake area behind the mountain. The Palace-City area includes the administration

office, printing house, living rooms for secular and Lama officials, prison and horse shed, etc. The Palace-Rooms area on the mountain top is a large group of buildings with the White Palace and the Red Palace as the main part. The White Palace is used to provide political and religious service for the Dalai Lama, and the top floor provides living quarters for him. The Red Palace is devoted to religion, and contains the tomb stupas of the Dalai Lamas of previous generations. The scripture chapels for religious activity are in the south of the White Palace and Red Palace.

1 | 2
1. 布达拉宫
   The Potala Palace
2. 布达拉宫外的转经桶
   Prayer wheels outside the Potala Palace

曲阜

Qufu

曲阜位于山东省西南部，它是中国历史文化名城，以"孔孟之乡、诗书之地、礼仪之邦"闻名于世。

曲阜是中国大思想家、教育家孔子的故乡。孔子创立的儒家学派，对中国几千年的封建文化产生了深远的影响。因此，历代统治者和封建文人对孔子非常崇敬，在这里建起了大型的孔府、孔庙、孔林（简称"三孔"）。

孔庙

孔庙位于曲阜城的中央。据史料记载，在孔子辞世的第二年，鲁哀公将孔子旧居改建为祭祀孔子的庙宇。后经历代重扩修建，在明代形成了现有规模。孔庙前后共九进院落，是我国规模仅次于故宫的古建筑群。孔庙内有孔子讲学的杏坛，还存有历代碑刻，被人们

视为书法、绘画和雕刻艺术的宝库。

孔府

孔府位于孔庙东侧，为孔子嫡系长子长孙的官署和私邸。现在的孔府基本上是明、清两代的建筑，包括厅、堂、楼、轩等480余间，共九进院落，前为官衙，后为内宅，是一座典型的中国贵族门户之家，有号称"天下第一人家"

的说法。府内存有著名的孔府档案和大量文物。

孔林

孔林位于曲阜城北部，为孔子及其后裔的墓地，占地3 000余亩。它是我国规模最大、持续年代最长、保存最完整的家族墓地和人工园林。孔子卒于鲁哀公十六年（公元前479年）四月乙丑，其后代将他葬在这里。从此以后，孔家后代从冢而葬，2 000多年从未间断。林内墓冢累累，多达10万余座，林内现有树木10万余株，碑刻4 000余块，著名文学家《桃花扇》的作者孔尚任的墓葬亦在此。

1 | 2

1. 孔府大门
   The main gate of the Kong Family Mansion
2. 孔子延生地——尼山夫子洞
   The Fuzi Cave on the Nishan Hill (the birthplace of Confucius)

Qufu

Qufu is located in the southwest of Shandong province. It is a famous historic and cultural city in China, known as "the hometown of Confucius and Mencius", "the place for literature" and "the state of etiquette".

Qufu is the birthplace of Confucius, the great thinker and educator of China. Confucius established Confucianism, which had a profound impact on Chinese feudal culture in the past thousands of years. Therefore, the rulers and feudal literati of the past dynasties worshiped Confucius. The large-scale Kong Family Mansion, the Temple of Confucius, and the Cemetery of Confucius (called "Three Kongs" for short) were set up in Qufu.

The Temple of Confucius

The Temple of Confucius is located in the center of Qufu city. According to historic records, within two years after the death of Confucius, his former house in Qufu was rebuilt to be consecrated as a temple by Lu Aigong, a king of the state of Lu. After the reconstruction and extension in later dynasties, it reached its current scale in the Ming Dynasty. In total, the Temple of Confucius consists of nine courtyards. It is the second largest historical building complex in China, second only to the Forbidden City. Inside the temple there is the Xingtan (Apricot Platform) where Confucius used to teach his students. Many stele inscriptions of the past dynasties are kept here, and therefore, the temple is considered the treasure house of calligraphy, painting and carving art.

The Kong Family Mansion

East of the Temple of Confucius lies the Kong Family Mansion where the eldest son and eldest grandson of the direct line of Confucius' descent lived and

worked. Most of the current mansion was built in the Ming and Qing Dynasties. It comprises over 480 halls, buildings and verandas with 9 courtyards. With offices in the front and a private residence in the back, it is a typical house for Chinese nobility. The mansion is honored as "the first house in the world". The archives of Confucius' family and a large amount of cultural relics are kept in the mansion.

The Cemetery of Confucius

Situated in the north of Qufu city, the Cemetery of Confucius is the graveyard for Confucius and his descendants. The cemetery encloses an area of over 3 000 mu (a Chinese measurement unit, equals 667 m^2). It is the largest and best-preserved family mausoleum and artificial garden with the longest history. Confucius died in the 16th year (479 BC) of the reign of Lu Aigong, and his descendants buried him there. From then on, Confucius' descendants never stopped the convention of being buried here for over 2 000 years. Today, there are more than 100 000 tombs in this cemetery with over 100 000 trees and 4 000 stele inscriptions. Kong Shangren, a famous writer and the author of "Peach Blossom Fan", is also buried there.

1 | 2　1. 孔林石雕
　　　　A stone statue of the Cemetery of the Kong Family
　　　2. 孔庙大成殿
　　　　The Dacheng Hall in the Temple of Confucius

221

泰山

Mount Taishan

泰山古名岱山，又称岱宗、岱岳、泰岳。它位于山东省中部泰安境内，是五岳（泰山、华山、衡山、嵩山、恒山）中的东岳，为五岳之首。1987年，被联合国教科文组织公布为世界自然与文化双遗产。

泰山是历代帝王封禅祭祀的山岳，具有崇高的地位。古代许多帝王都在泰山进行封禅活动。据说汉武帝7次到泰山，乾隆10次到泰山。封建帝王视泰山为神的化身，来泰山封禅祭祀，因而庙宇题刻、古寺亭桥遍布山间。

玉皇顶

玉皇顶是泰山最高峰，海拔1 524米。山顶上有玉皇庙，古时候登山祭天就在这里设祭坛。这里也是看日出和云海的好地方。

你知道吗？ Do you know?

在登泰山的途中，有个闻名中外的经石峪。在斜坡石壁上，刻隶书《金刚经》经文，原来有 2 500 多字，经过 1 400 多年的风吹雨打，现在还残存 1 043 个字。每个字有 50 厘米见方，被人们誉为"大字鼻祖"。

On the way to the top of Mount Taishan, there is a world-renowned *Jingshiyu*. On the stone walls of the slopes, Jingang Scripture (a Buddhist classic work) is carved in official script (an ancient style of calligraphy current in the Han Dynasty). There used to be over 2 500 characters. After 1 400 years' wind and rain, there are still 1 043 characters left, each being 50 cm square. The inscription is praised as"the ancestor of big characters".

南天门

南天门又称"三天门"，是登泰山的最后一道门坊，也是泰山顶的大门。

岱庙

泰山的古代建筑特别多，山下的岱庙是中国历代皇帝拜"泰山神"的地方。岱庙坊在岱庙的正阳门外，古代帝王来泰山祭祀首先在这里举行简短仪式，然后才到岱庙举行正式大祭。

大观殿是岱庙的主殿，建于宋代，是古代帝王来泰山祭祀"泰山神"的地方。主殿的殿壁上有幅巨型壁画，长 62 米，高 3.3 米，描绘了"泰山神"出巡和归来的场景，是件艺术珍品。

1 | 2
1. 泰山美景
   Mount Taishan
2. 南天门
   The South Heaven Gate

Mount Taishan

Mount Taishan is called Mount Daishan in ancient times. It is also called Daizong, Daiyue or Taiyue. Situated in Tai'an in central Shandong Province, Mount Taishan is the easternmost mountain and takes the lead in the five sacred mountains. In 1987, UNESCO listed it as one of the world natural, as well as cultural heritage sites.

The sublime position of Mount Taishan was conferred by emperors of past dynasties who frequently went there to pay homage and offer sacrifices to heaven and earth. Many ancient emperors have been there for times. For example, Emperor Wu of the Han Dynasty had been to Mount Taishan seven times, and Emperor Qianlong had been there ten times. Feudal emperors who paid homage to Mount Taishan regarded the mountain as god's incarnation. The whole mountain is abundant in inscriptions, old temples, pavilions and bridges.

The Peak of the Jade Emperor

The Peak of the Jade Emperor is the highest peak of Mount Taishan with an altitude of 1 524 m. On the summit there is the Temple of the Jade Emperor. In ancient times, people would scale the mountain and set up sacrificial altars to offer sacrifices to heaven. It is also a good place to view the sunrise and sea of cloud.

The South Heaven Gate

The South Heaven Gate, also called the Three-Heaven Gate, is the last archway before climbing onto the summit of Mount Taishan. It is also the gate to the mountain summit.

The Temple to the God of Mount Taishan

Among the numerous ancient buildings on Mount Taishan, the

Temple to the God of Mount Taishan at the foot of Mount Taishan is the place where Chinese emperors of every dynasty worshipped the God of Mount Taishan. The Memorial Arch of the Temple to the God of Mount Taishan is outside of the Zhengyang Gate. In ancient times, emperors would hold a short and simple rite here before they held the formal ceremony of offering sacrifices within the temple.

The Heavenly Grant Palace, the main palace of the Temple to the God of Mount Taishan, was built in the Song Dynasty (960 — 1279 AD). It is a place where ancient emperors offered sacrifices to the God of Mount Taishan. On the wall is a huge mural 62 m long and 3.3 m high. It is a rare work of art representing how the God of Mount Taishan went on a tour of inspection.

	2	
1		3

1. 玉皇顶
   The Peak of Jade Emperor
2. 岱庙坊
   The Memorial Arch of the Dai Temple
3. 岱顶石刻 "五岳独尊"
   Inscription on the summit of Mount Taishan

▶ 你知道吗？ Do you know?

北京的故宫、曲阜的孔庙和岱庙被誉为中国三大宫殿建筑群。

The Palace Museum of Beijing, the Confucius Temple of Qufu and the Temple to the God of Mount Taishan are reputed to be the three great palace complexes.

嵩山

Mount Songshan

嵩山位于河南省中部，是"五岳"中的中岳，主要由太室山和少室山组成。

嵩山有72座山峰，山峰奇特，山色秀丽。最高峰是太室山的主峰峻极峰，高度为1 440米。山上有古建筑群18处，其中中岳庙、少林寺、嵩阳书院、塔林、观星台等最为著名。山下有72座寺庙，是佛教、道教、儒教三教汇集的地方，庙内文物众多，有"文物之乡"的美称。

中岳庙

中岳庙在秦朝开始修建，是古代帝王祭祀山神的地方，占地10万余平方米，大小殿阁楼亭有400多间，是"五岳"中现存规模最大、最完整的古代建筑群。

少林寺

少室山上的少林寺，在唐朝时被称为"天下第一名刹"，是中国佛教禅宗发源地。少林武功更是闻名世界，被奉为"武林之尊"。

▶ 小资料 Data

千佛殿是少林寺内规模最大的殿堂。殿内的三面墙上有大型的彩色壁画，面积300多平方米，为著名唐代画家吴道子所作。

少林寺的塔林，是历代和尚的墓塔，现在有220多座，是中国现存最大的塔林。塔的大小、形状各不相同，有圆柱形、锥形、瓶形。有的高达7~8米，有的只有1米左右。

嵩阳书院

嵩阳书院是历史悠久、规模宏大的官办书院，是中国古代四大书院之一。

Mount Songshan

Mount Songshan, situated in central Henan Province, stands in the middle position among the five sacred mountains. It is mainly comprised of Taishi Mountain and Shaoshi Mountain.

Mount Songshan has 72 peculiar and elegant peaks. The highest peak is the Junji Hill (1440 m), the main peak of Taishi Mountain. There are 18 ancient architectural complexes, among which the Zhongyue Temple, the Shaolin Temple, the Songyang Academy, the Forest of Pagodas and the Guanxing (Observing Stars) Terrace are the most famous ones. At the foot of Mount Songshan, there are 72 temples of Buddhism, Taoism and Confucianism with a huge collection of cultural relics, earning the area a reputation as "the land of cultural relics".

The Zhongyue Temple

The Zhongyue Temple was built in the Qin Dynasty. With an area

"五岳" 指中国五大名山，它们分别是东岳泰山、西岳华山、中岳嵩山、南岳衡山、北岳恒山。

The five sacred mountains refer to the five most famous mountains in China. They are the Eastern Mount Taishan, the Western Mount Huashan, the Central Mount Songshan, the Southern Mount Hengshan and the Northern Mount Hengshan.

of more than 100 000 m², it is the place where the ancient emperors offered sacrifices to the god of mountains. The temple consists of 400 halls, verandas, towers and pavilions. It is the largest and most complete ancient architectural complex in the famous "five sacred mountains".

The Shaolin Temple

The Shaolin Temple on the Shaoshi Mountain was called the most famous temple in the Tang Dynasty. It is also the birthplace of Zen Buddhism. Shaolin Kung Fu is held in the highest regard among the martial arts circles all over the world.

The Thousand Buddha Hall is the largest hall in the Shaolin Temple. The hall's three sides bear large colorful wall murals with an area of over 300 m². The murals were painted by Wu Daozi, a famous Tang Dynasty painter.

The Forest of Pagodas contains more than 220 monuments to noted monks from years gone by. It is the biggest extant forest of pagodas in China. The pagodas here vary in size and shape. Some are cylindrical, some cones, while others are like jars. Some of the pagodas are 7 to 8 m tall, while some are just around 1 m.

The Songyang Academy

The Songyang Academy was a big academy established by the government. With its long history, it is one of the four most famous ancient academies in Chinese history.

1 | 2

1. 塔林
   The Forest of Pagodas
2. 中岳庙中的铁人
   The iron statues of the Zhongyue Temple

229

黄山

Mount Huangshan

黄山位于安徽省南部，是中国著名的风景旅游区和疗养避暑胜地，被誉为国之瑰宝、世界奇观，1990年被联合国教科文组织列入世界自然和文化遗产名录。

黄山素有"中国第一奇山"之誉，险峻、雄伟、奇特、壮观。千米以上的高峰有77座，著名的山峰有30座。最高峰是莲花峰，海拔高度为1 873米；其次为天都峰和光明顶，高度都超过了1 800米。

黄山以"奇松、怪石、云海、温泉"四绝闻名于世。

奇松

黄山的松树大多生长在悬崖峭壁上，扎根在悬岩裂缝中，千姿百态，奇妙绝伦，非常惹人喜爱。

黄山最著名的松树是"迎

1 | 2　1. 黄山
　　　　Mount Huangshan
　　　2. 飞来石
　　　　The Feilai Rock

▶ 小资料　Data

黄山风景区方圆154平方千米，号称"五百里黄山"。

在黄山特产中，名茶"黄山毛峰"和名药"灵芝草"驰名中外。

The Mount Huangshan has an area of about 154 km², known as 500-li (0.5 km) Mount Huangshan.

Among the local special products of Mount Huangshan, the green tea Mao Feng (the downy tips of the tea leaves) and the magic fungus (a Chinese herb medicine) are world-famous.

客松"。它破石而生，挺立在玉屏峰东侧、文殊洞之上，已生长了千年以上。它树枝前伸，就像人伸开手臂迎接远方的客人。

怪石

黄山的怪石特别多，如莲花峰的岩石呈莲花瓣形状，从远处看它像一朵初开的莲花；飞来石位于飞来峰，底部和山峰似乎截然分开，好像是从天外飞来的一样；在北海散花坞左侧，有一块孤立石峰，顶巅长了棵奇松像花一样，故名"梦笔生花"。

还有如"松鼠跳天都"、"猴子观海"、"天女散花"、"关公挡曹"、"仙人卜棋"等，个个都形象逼真，使游客流连忘返。

云海

黄山四季都有壮观的云海，每当云海出现时，山峰时隐时现，特别是夕阳斜照而有云雾时，有时会出现一种彩色的光环。人在光环之中，人动影亦动，这就是著名的"宝光"，也叫"佛光"。

温泉

前山温泉是黄山最著名的温泉，每隔若干年，水色就会变红，经过六七天后方逐渐变清。其水温一般在42℃，水质清澈，可以饮用，可以沐浴，具有医疗价值。

Mount Huangshan

Mount Huangshan, situated in the south of Anhui Province, is a famous scenic spot and convalescent and summer resort in China. It is honored as a national treasure and a wonder in the world. In 1990, UNESCO listed it as a world natural and cultural heritage site.

Mount Huangshan, precipitous and magnificent, is usually considered as the most peculiar mountain in China. There are 77 peaks over 1 000 m high, 30 of which are very famous. The highest one is the Lotus Peak (1 873 m), followed by the Peak of Celestial City and the Peak of Brightness, both above 1 800 m.

The renowned Four Wonders of Huangshan are the spectacular rocks, oddly shaped pines, hot springs and the sea of cloud.

The Peculiar Pine Trees

Pine trees of Mount Huangshan mainly grow on the cliffs or are rooted in the cracks between rocks. They are different in posture, but all are incomparably marvelous and adorable.

The most famous pine tree on Mount Huangshan is the so-called Guests-Greeting Pine Tree which comes out of rocks and stands upright over the Cave of Wisdom east of the Peak of the Jade Screen. It has been there for more than 1 000 years. Its front branches stretch forward as if it is spreading its arms to greet guests from afar.

The spectacular Rocks

There are numerous spectacular rocks on Mount Huangshan such

▶ 你知道吗？ Do you know?

黄山自然风景优美，明代地理学家、旅行家徐霞客发出了"薄海内外无如徽之黄山，登黄山，天下无山，观止矣"的感叹。

Mount Huangshan has wonderful scenery Xu Xiake, a famous geographer and traveler of the Ming Dynasty (1368-1644), visited the mountain, and described it in a poem, calling it the best of all mountains. The poem goes to the effects that no mountain in the world could bear comparison with Mount Huangshan; no mountain in the world deserves climbing after one visiting Mount Huangshan.

▶ 小知识 Knowledge

因为黄山山峰的石壁是黑色的，所以在秦朝的时候被称为黟山，意思是黑山。相传轩辕黄帝在此炼丹成仙，后来信奉道教的唐明皇下令将黟山改称为黄山，意思是黄帝之山，别称"黄岳"。

Because the cliffs of Mount Huangshan are black, they were originally called the Yishan (Black Mountain) in the Qin Dynasty. It is said that the Yellow Emperor Xuanyuan (legendary ancestor of the Chinese nation) made elixirs here and became an immortal. Later, Emperor Ming of the Tang Dynasty, who believed in Taoism, issued an edict renaming the Yishan as Mount Huangshan to commemorate the Yellow Emperor. The mountain is also called Huangyue (Yellow Mountain).

as rocks on the Lotus Peak which look like a lotus in blossom when seen from far away and the Feilai Rock (a rock dropped from the sky) on the Feilai Peak (peak that appears out of nowhere) which seems to be separated from the peak, as if it alighted from afar.

At the left side of the Valley of the North Sea Disseminating Flowers, there is an isolated rock peak on the top of which grows a peculiar pine tree like a flower, known as "Dreamy Blossom".

In addition, there are rocks like Squirrel Jumping over the Celestial City, Donkey Viewing the Sea, Celestial Girls Scattering Flowers, Lord Guan Blocking the Way of Cao Cao, Immortals Playing Chess and so on, each of which looks vivid, attracting tourists with their peculiar charm.

The Sea of Cloud

There is splendid sea of cloud on Mount Huangshan. When the sea of cloud appears, peaks emerge and disappear from time to time. Especially at sunset, a colorful aureole occasionally occurs. The aureole may encircle people and move with people's stirring. This is the famous "treasure light", also called "Buddha's halo".

Hot Springs

The hot spring in the front part of Mount Huangshan is the most famous kind. In an interval of a few years, the water turns red before gradually clearing after six or seven days. Its temperature usually stays at 42 ℃ The water is limpid, and is suitable for drinking and showering. It is of some medicinal value.

1. 云海
   The sea of cloud
2. 迎客松
   The Guest-Greeting Pine Tree

庐山

Mount Lushan

庐山位于江西九江市南，北边有长江，东边有鄱阳湖，交通便利，以"雄、奇、险、秀"闻名于世，风景优美，气势雄伟，是闻名中外的旅游和避暑胜地，现已被联合国教科文组织列入世界文化遗产名录。

庐山的每座山峰都巍峨挺拔，雄伟壮观，山间经常充满云雾。主峰汉阳峰海拔1 474米。

庐山景点非常多，著名的有三叠泉、龙首崖、三宝树、五老峰、仙人洞、含鄱口等。

三叠泉

三叠泉是"庐山第一奇观"，高100多米，依山体分为上、中、下三级，所以又叫"三级泉"。它从高高的山上凌空下泻，就像水帘悬挂在空中，因此又称它为"水帘泉"。

含鄱口

含鄱口位于含鄱岭上，面对鄱阳湖，是看日出的好地方。

三宝树

三宝树是三棵高耸入云的古树，相传是晋朝人种植的。一棵是银杏树，另外两棵是柳杉树。

Mount Lushan

1. 庐山
   Mount Lushan

2. 三叠泉
   The Three-fold Spring

▶ 你知道吗？ Do you know?

庐山是著名的避暑胜地。在烈日炎炎的七月，平均气温只有22℃，早晚更加凉爽。山中别墅很多，现存具有英、美、法、俄、德等多个国家建筑风格的别墅总数为636幢，它们大多用庐山之石建成。

Mount Lushan is a famous summer resort. In sweltering July, its average temperature is only 22℃. It is even cooler in the morning and at night. There are 636 villas on the mountains, which are of the architectural styles of Britain, America, France, Russia and Germany. They are mostly built with the stones from Mount Lushan.

Mount Lushan has convenient transportation. Situated in the south of Jiujiang City in Jiangxi Province, it is bordered on the north by the Yangtze River and on the east by the Poyang Lake. It earns its fame with its grandiosity, peculiarity, perilousness and elegance. With beautiful scenery and cool summers, it is a world-renowned summer resort and a world cultural heritage site listed by UNESCO.

Each peak of Mount Lushan is towering and splendid, and the misty clouds blanket the valleys. The Hanyang Peak, the main peak of Mount Lushan, stands 1 474 m above sea level.

There are many attractions on Mount Lushan, such as the famous Three-fold Spring, the Cliff of the Dragon's Head, the Three-precious Trees, the Five-elder Peak, the Immortal Cave, the Hanpo Entrance, etc.

The Three-fold Spring

The Three-fold Spring is the "first marvelous spectacle of Mount Lushan". Over 100 m tall, it is divided into three levels along the mountain, i.e. the upper, middle and lower levels. So it is also called "Three-Level Spring". It pours down from the high mountain like a water curtain hanging in the air, so it has another name — the "Water Curtain Spring".

The Hanpo Entrance

The Hanpo Entrance, located on Hanpo Peak, faces the Poyang Lake and is a good place to watch the sunrise.

The Three-Precious Trees

The Three-Treasure Trees are three ancient trees towering into the sky. It is believed that they were planted by people in the Jin Dynasty (265 — 420 AD). One is ginkgo and the other two are cryptomerias.

▶ 小资料 Data

相传殷、周间，有匡氏兄弟结伴到庐山修行，因此庐山也称匡庐。

It is said that during the period between the Yin and Zhou dynasties there were brothers of the Kuang Family who came to Mount Lushan to cultivate themselves in order to attain immortality, so Mount Lushan is also called Kuang Lu.

武夷山

Mount Wuyi

武夷山位于福建省西北部，是福建省最高峰。这里碧水丹山，奇险秀丽，自古就以"奇秀甲东南"著称于世，现已被联合国教科文组织列入世界自然和文化双遗产名录，被称为"世界生物之窗"。

武夷山共有36座山峰，造型奇特，千姿百态，引人入胜，包括三仰峰、大王峰、玉女峰、天游峰等。武夷山风景区主要由九曲溪、天游峰、桃源洞、天心岩、武夷宫、水帘洞、虎啸岩和莲花峰等景点组成。

九曲溪

武夷山的精华在九曲溪。九曲溪就是溪水共弯九曲，全长约 7.5 千米，溪水碧清，曲曲弯弯，武夷山著名的山峰都列在溪

边。乘竹筏游九曲溪，可以看两岸的美景，这是游武夷山最精彩的节目。

玉女峰

玉女峰是武夷山最迷人、最秀丽的山峰，就像仙女下凡一样，屹立在九曲溪边。

大王峰

大王峰端庄雄伟，具有王者风范，所以人们都叫它"大王峰"。山峰顶大腰细，仿佛是顶纱帽，又称它为纱帽岩。大王峰四壁陡峭，只能从一条裂缝中的爬梯登上山顶。

天游峰

天游峰为"武夷第一胜地"。这里云雾多，是看云海的最佳地方，在峰顶可以看到九曲溪全景。

Mount Wuyi

Mount Wuyi, situated in the northwest of Fujian Province, is the highest mount in Fujian. It has green water and red peaks that are fantastic, precipitous, elegant and beautiful. Since ancient times, it has enjoyed the reputation of being "the most marvelous and elegant mountain in the southeast". UNESCO listed it as a world natural as well as cultural heritage. It is eulogized as a "biological showcase of the world".

Mount Wuyi contains 36 peculiar and attractive peaks that adopt different postures. The main ones are the Three-Admiration Peak, the Great King Peak, the Jade Lady Peak, the Heavenly Tour Peak and so on. The scenic attractions include the Nine-Curve Stream, the Heavenly Tour Peak, the Land of Peach Blossom Cave, the Heaven's Heart Rock, the Wuyi Palace, the Water Curtain Cave, the Tiger Growl Cave and the Lotus Peak, etc.

The Nine-Curve Stream

The essence of Mount Wuyi is the Nine-Curve Stream, famous for its nine curves. The stream is jade green and crystal clear, winding its way among the mountains. A bamboo raft will take you on a 7.5km cruise down the meandering Nine-Curve Stream with all the gorgeous scenery on both banks. This would be the most exciting moment in your tour to Mount Wuyi.

Jade Lady Peak

Jade Lady Peak, the most charming and elegant peak of Mount Wuyi, looks like a fairy descending from heaven to the earth. It is located by the Nine-Curve Stream.

Great King Peak

The grand and solemn Great King Peak has the demeanor of a king, hence its name. The peak's top is wider than its middle part, resembling a gauze hat (a hat worn by an official in old times), so it is also called "the Gauze Hat Rock". Four sides of the peak are all precipitous cliffs. There is only one way through a crevice to the summit.

Heavenly Tour Peak

Heavenly Tour Peak is the best place to view the sea of cloud. From the top you can also have a panoramic view of the Nine-Curve Stream.

1. 武夷山
   Mount Wuyi
2. 玉女峰
   Jade Lady Peak

▶ 你知道吗? Do you know?

武夷山既是千年文化名山，又是道教的发源地之一。

Mount Wuyi is a famous mountain with more than a thousand years of history and culture. It it is also one of the original places of Taoism.

237

武当山

Mount Wudang

武当山玉虚岩
The hollow-jade-rock of Mount Wudang

▶ 小资料　Data

唐代太宗李世民于贞观年间（627—649年）修建了五龙祠。到宋代，直接为皇室服务的武当道教基本形成。到了明代，武当道教达到鼎盛时期，成为至高无上的皇室家庙、全国道教活动中心。

Li Shimin, Emperor Taizong of the Tang Dynasty, had the Five Dragon Temple built in the period of Zhenguan(624–649 AD). In the Song Dynasty, Wudang Taoism, which served only the imperial family, was basically formed. It reached its zenith in the Ming Dynasty when the huge temple complex on Mount Wudang became the supreme temples for the royal family, enjoying the name of Taoistic center of the country.

　　武当山位于湖北省西北部，是著名的道教胜地之一。山峦清秀，风景清幽。大小山峰共有72座，主峰天柱峰海拔1 612米。武当山现已被联合国教科文组织列入世界文化遗产名录。

　　武当山拥有众多的自然胜景和人文胜景，主要包括三潭、九泉、九井、九台、十池、十石、十一洞、二十四洞、三十六崖和七十二峰等。山上古代建筑中规模宏伟、工程浩大的道教宫观，是世界古代建筑史上的奇迹。

　　建于天柱峰绝顶的金殿又称金顶，总重约90吨，是中国现有最大的铜建筑物之一。

Mount Wudang

Mount Wudang, located in the northwest of Hubei Province, is one of the famous holy places of Taoism as well as one of the world cultural heritage sites listed by UNESCO. The mountains are elegant and the landscape is quiet and beautiful. There are altogether 72 peaks, among which the main peak, Heaven Pillar Peak, stands tallest at 1 612 m above sea level.

Mount Wudang has plenty of scenic and historic sites, including three ponds, nine springs, nine wells, nine terraces, ten lakes, ten rocks, eleven caves, twenty-four caves, thirty-six cliffs and seventy-two peaks. With a tremendous amount of work, the Taoist temples look grandiose among the ancient architecture on Mount Wudang, and are a miracle in the history of ancient architecture in the world.

The Golden Palace on the top of the Heaven Pillar Peak is also called the Golden Summit. Weighing about 90 tons, it is one of the largest copper buildings in China.

▶ 小资料 Data

传说道教信奉的 "真武大帝" 即在此修仙得道飞升。

According to the legend, the Taoist deity Zhenwu practiced alchemy and attained immortality atop the mountain.

▶ 你知道吗？ Do you know?

武当山是武当派拳术发源地，以 "武当太乙五行拳" 闻名中外。

令武当山真正名扬天下的是一代宗师张三丰，他创立的武当派与嵩山少林派齐名。武当派武术与道教渊源极深，它讲究以柔克刚，后发制人，自成一派，被称为 "内家拳派"。

Mount Wudang is the cradle of Wudang Boxing, which is renowned in the world for the "Wudang Taiyi Five Elements Boxing".

Created by the martial arts exponent Zhang Sanfeng, Wudang Kung Fu is connected with Taoism. It is centered on the principle of conquering toughness by gentleness, mainly using the opponent's initiation to gain mastery. This is a distinct type of martial arts and is called internal Kung Fu. The Wudang Faction founded by Zhang Sanfeng is considered to be on a par with the Shaolin Faction.

五台山

Mount Wutai

五台山位于山西省东北部，是中国四大佛教名山之一。

五台山有五座高大的山峰，它们是北台叶斗峰、东台望海峰、西台挂月峰、南台锦绣峰、中台翠岩峰。最高峰是叶斗峰，海拔 3 058 米。

五台山寺庙很多，共有 58 座。最著名的有 5 处，分别是塔院寺、显通寺、殊像寺、罗睺寺和菩萨顶。它们的建筑非常有特色，是中国古代建筑的精华。

五台山是文殊菩萨的道场。

显通寺

显通寺是五台山历史最久、规模最大的寺庙。它建于汉代，人们称它为"祖寺"。

▶ 小资料　Data

"灵峰胜境"菩萨顶有一座"滴水殿"，有趣的是，不管天晴还是下雨，宝殿四檐都是雨珠下滴，天长日久，檐台的石条上被滴出一排排深坑。

On the Peak of the Bodhisattva, there is a Hall of Dripping Water. The funny thing is that, no matter whether it is sunny or rainy, there is always rain dripping from the eaves of the hall. After a considerable period of time rows of trenches appear on the stone slates.

▶ 小知识　Knowledge

菩萨顶有个"万人斋"用的大铜锅。猜猜看，这大铜锅究竟有多大？据说，僧人吃过饭后，锅底的锅巴要用大黄牛拉犁来耕呢！

There is a huge copper pot used to contain ten thousand people's meal in the Temple of the Bodhisattva. Can you imagine how big the pot is? It is said that after monks finished their meals, the rice crust left in the pot needed to be ploughed out by a strong ox!

Mount Wutai

Mount Wutai, situated in the northeast of Shanxi Province, is one of the four famous mountains of Buddhism in China.

There are five lofty peaks on Mount Wutai, namely the Northern Peak of Yedou, Eastern Peak of Viewing the Sea, Western Peak of Hanging Moon, Southern Peak of Charm and Middle Peak of Green Rock. The highest peak is the Peak of Yedou which is 3 058 m above sea level.

There are altogether 58 temples on Mount Wutai. The most famous are the Temple of Pagoda Courtyard, the Temple of Revealing Comprehension, the Temple of the Statue of Manjusri, the Temple of Luohou and the Temple of the Bodhisattva. The temples have distinctive styles and are the essence of Chinese ancient architecture.

Mount Wutai is where Buddhist rites of the Bodhisattva Manjusri were performed.

The Temple of Revealing Comprehension

The Temple of Revealing Comprehension is the biggest temple with the longest history on Mount Wutai. Built in the Han Dynasty (206 BC — 220 AD), it is called the "Ancestral Temple".

峨眉山

Mount Emei

峨眉山位于四川省境内，是中国四大佛教名山之一。峨眉山青峰叠翠，风景秀丽，有"峨眉天下秀"的美誉。峨眉山及附近的乐山大佛，已被联合国教科文组织列入世界自然和文化遗产。

峨眉山是供奉普贤菩萨的佛山。山中寺庙很多，主要有报国寺、伏虎寺、万年寺，其中规模最大、最宏伟的是报国寺。

金顶

峨眉山的金顶海拔为3 077米，在金顶上看"佛光"是游人的愿望，"佛光"使峨眉山富有神秘色彩，能看到"佛光"的游客都感到万分荣幸。

每当天空晴朗，没有风的时候，在下午两三点钟以后，人们站在金顶的舍身崖上，俯身下望，有时会看到五彩光环浮于云际，自己的身影置于光

环之中，影随人移，互不相叠。无论有多少人并排观看，他们所有到的始终是自己的身影。过去，人们解释不了这种现象，认为是"佛光"。其实，这不过是太阳光、云层和人体三者处在45°斜线上的时候所产生的折射现象。

伏虎寺的传说

宋朝时，该寺叫神龙堂。后来，寺庙附近出现了猛虎，经常伤人，庙里的和尚建立了 尊胜幢，从此以后，老虎没有了，寺名就改为伏虎寺。

▶ 你知道吗？ *Do you know?*

万年寺的骑象菩萨重62吨，高7.3米。它已经有1 000多年的历史。

The statue of the Bodhisattva riding on elephant in the Ten-Thousand-Year Temple weighs 62 tons and stands 7.3 m. It has been there for over 1 000 years.

1	2

1. 峨眉山
   Mount Emei
2. 佛光
   The Buddha's halo

Mount Emei

Mount Emei, situated in Sichuan Province, is one of the four famous mountains of Buddhism in China. Green mountains undulate and trees overlap each other on Mount Emei, giving it the reputation as "the most graceful mountain in China". It was inscribed by the UNESCO on the world natual and cultural heritage list.

Mount Emei is a Buddhist mountain enshrining the Bodhisattva of Universal Benevolence. There are many temples on the mountain, including the Baoguosi Temple, the Tiger-Taming Temple and the Ten-Thousand-Year Temple. Among them, the biggest and most magnificent one is the Baoguosi Temple.

The Golden Peak

The Golden Peak of Mount Emei is 3 077 m above sea level. To view the "Buddha's halo" is the wish of many tourists. The "Buddha's halo" gives Mount Emei a touch of mystery. Those who see the halo feel lucky and honored.

When it is sunny and windless, after two or three o'clock in the afternoon, if you stand on the Sheshen Cliff of the Golden Peak and look down, you may sometimes see a colorful aureole floating over the clouds. Your body will appear in the aureole. When you move, the aureole moves with you. No matter how many people stand together viewing it, they invariably see their own shadows alone. In the past, people couldn't explain this phenomenon and thought it was Buddha's halo. Now we know it is actually a phenomenon of refraction, which occurs when sunlight, cloud layers and human body form an angle of 45 degrees.

The Legend of the Tiger-Taming Temple

In the Song Dynasty, the Tiger-Taming Temple was called the Hall of the Magical Dragon. Later, ferocious tigers appeared near the temple and often attacked people. So the monks set up a holy pillar inscribed with the name of the Buddha. After that, the tigers disappeared and the temple was renamed the Tiger-Taming Temple.

1. 金顶
   The Golden Peak
2. 万年寺
   The Ten-Thousand-Year Temple

▶ 小资料 Data

报国寺是在明朝时候修建的。寺内有一尊巨大的瓷佛，高 2.47 米，是 1415 年在景德镇烧制的，为稀世珍品。

The Baoguosi Temple was built in the Ming Dynasty. In the temple there is a huge porcelain statue of the Buddha, standing 2.47m high. Made in Jingdezhen (a place known as the "Ceramics Metropolis"of China) in 1415, it is considered a rare treasure in the world.

乐山大佛

The Giant Buddha in Leshan

　　乐山大佛是中国唐代的佛教石刻造像，位置在四川省乐山市东面，岷江、青衣江、大渡河交汇处的栖鸾峰下，是在凌云山山崖上凿成的。

　　大佛为弥勒佛坐像，通高71米，肩宽24米。其中头高14.7米、宽10米，耳朵长6.7米，眼睛长3.3米，脖子高3米，脚背宽9米，它是世界上最大的石刻佛像，可以说"山是一尊佛，佛是一座山"。

The Giant Buddha in Leshan

The Giant Buddha in Leshan, chiseled out on the cliff of the Lingyun Mountain, is located at the foot of Qiluan Peak where the Minjiang, Qingyijiang and Daduhe rivers converge to the east of Leshan City, Sichuan Province. It is a stone carving statue of Buddha made in the Tang Dynasty.

The 71m-tall statue of the Laughing Buddha is in a sitting posture. Its head is 14.7 m tall and 10 m wide; its shoulders are 24 m wide; its ears are 6.7 m long; its eyes are 3.3 m long; the neck is 3 m tall; and its foot instep is 9 m wide. It is the biggest stone carving statue in the world. Hence goes the saying that "the entire cliff is a giant Buddha and the Buddha dominates the cliff".

1 | 2

1. 乐山大佛
   The Giant Buddha in Leshan
2. 大佛侧面像
   The profile of the Giant Buddha

▶ 你知道吗？ Do you know?

大佛的脚背上可以围坐 100 多人。

More than 100 persons can sit simultaneously on the bare foot of the Giant Buddha of Leshan.

普陀山

Mount Putuo

普陀山是浙江省东部舟山群岛中的一座山岛，是中国四大佛教名山之一，有"海天佛国"之称，也是著名的旅游胜地。

普陀山是以山水优美著称的名山，这里山海相连，景色秀丽雄伟。主峰佛顶山海拔290余米，是全岛最高峰。岛上寺院庵堂众多，古木参天；海边岩沙相间，海潮如带；岛上气候温和，四季宜人。

普陀山名胜古迹很多，以普济寺、法雨寺、慧济寺三寺为主的建筑群最具代表性，其中普济寺最大。

普济寺

普济寺始建于宋朝，是供奉观音菩萨的主刹，建筑总面积 11 000 多平方米。寺内有大圆通殿、天王殿、藏经殿、钟鼓楼等。

Mount Putuo

Mount Putuo is an island of hills among the Zhoushan Archipelago east of Zhejiang Province. It is one of the four famous mountains of Buddhism and has a reputation of being "the Buddhist resort of the sea and sky". It is also a famous tourist resort.

Mount Putuo is famous for its scenic landscapes. Its hills merge with the sea and form picturesque and grandiose scenes. Buddha Top Mountain, the main peak of the island, stands tallest at over 290 m. There are a large number of temples, nunneries, and prayer halls. Ancient trees here stretch out to reach the sky. On the beach the rocks alternate with sand, and sea tides rise and fall. The climate on the mountain is mild and comfortable all year round.

There are many scenic and historical sites on Mount Putuo. The most typical one is the building complex consisting mainly of the Puji Temple, the Fayu Temple and the Huiji Temple. Of the three temples, the Puji Temple is the biggest one.

The Puji Temple

The Puji Temple, originally built in the Song Dynasty, is the main monastery for worshipping the Goddess of Mercy. It covers a floor space of more than 11 000 m². In it there are the Hall of Great Flexibility, the Hall of Celestial King, the Tripitaka Hall, the Tower of Bell and Drum, etc.

1 | 2

1. 南海观音像
   The statue of the Goddess of Mercy
2. 多宝塔
   The Duobao Pagoda

九华山

Mount Jiuhua

九华山
Mount Jiuhua

九华山位于安徽省西南部，是中国四大佛教名山之一，有"香火甲天下"、"东南第一山"之称，进香朝拜的中外游客终年络绎不绝。

九华山自然风光十分秀美，有99座山峰，以天台、莲花、天柱、十王等九峰最为雄伟，主峰十王峰海拔1 341米，是九华山最高点。

九华山气候宜人，名刹古寺林立，与自然风景巧妙结合，被称为"莲花佛国"、"佛国仙城"。九华山有化城寺、肉身宝殿、百岁宫等大小寺庙82座，大小佛像6 800多尊，是善男信女的朝拜圣地和旅游避暑胜地。

化城寺

化城寺是九华山的主寺，781年被辟为地藏道场，当时皇帝赐匾额"化城寺"。寺内藏有许多经文，是国家稀有文物。

肉身宝殿

相传肉身宝殿藏有地藏菩萨的肉身，殿内有许多佛教珍贵文物。

百岁宫

百岁宫又叫万年寺，是为了供奉无瑕禅师的真身而修建的。无瑕禅师来九华山修行

▶ 你知道吗？ Do you know?

九华山有棵凤凰古松，已经生长了1 400多年，是九华山一大胜景。

On Mount Jiuhua there is an ancient phoenix pine tree that has lived for over 1 400 years. It is a marvelous scene on Mount Jiuhua.

Mount Jiuhua

时才 26 岁，长年以野果、泉水为生，活到 126 岁，坐化而死。死后 3 年，身体保存完好。现在，殿内所供奉的是无瑕禅师的真身。

▶ 小资料　Data

古新罗国(今朝鲜半岛东南部)高僧金乔觉来九华山修行，99 岁圆寂，3 年肉身不烂，人们认为他是地藏菩萨转世。从此，九华山成为地藏菩萨的道场。

In ancient times, Jin Qiaojue, an eminent monk from today's Southeastern Korean Peninsula came to Mount Jiuhua to practice Buddhism. At the age of 99, he passed away, but his body remained intact for three years. He was re-spected as the incarnation of the Earth Store Bodhisattva. From then on, Mount Jiuhua became a place where Bud-dhist rites of the Earth Store Bodhisattva were performed.

Mount Jiuhua, situated in the southwest of Anhui Province, is one of the four famous Buddhist mountains in China, with the reputation of "the busiest pilgrimage place in China" and "the number one mountain in the Southeast". It attracts numerous domestic and foreign tourists to burn incense and tender their worship all year round.

Mount Jiuhua has very beautiful natural scenery. There are 99 peaks, among which the nine peaks of the Heavenly Terrace, the Lotus Glory, the Heavenly Pillar, the Ten Kings and so on are the most magnificent. The main Peak of Ten Kings is 1 341 m above sea level, and its summit is the highest point of Mount Jiuhua.

Mount Jiuhua is endowed with a pleasant weather. Its numerous ancient temples integrate naturally with the graceful landscape. It is reputed to be "the Buddhist country of lotus" and "the Buddhist land of the immortals". There are 82 temples, such as the Huacheng Temple, the Treasure Hall of Corporeal Body, the One-Hundred-Year Palace, and over 6 800 Buddhist statues of various sizes. It is a sanctum for devotees to worship and also a summer resort for tourists.

Huacheng Temple

Huacheng Temple is the main temple of Mount Jiuhua. In 781 AD, it was opened as a place where Buddhist rites of the Earth Store Bodhisattva were performed. At that time, the emperor granted a horizontal board bearing three Chinese characters: Hua Cheng Temple. A large collection of rare Buddhist scriptures is housed in the temple which are rare cultural relics of the country.

Precious Hall of Corporeal Body

It is said that the corporeal body

转轮宝殿
The Zhuanlun Hall

of the Earth Store Bodhisattva is kept in this hall, along with many precious Buddhist cultural relics.

The One-Hundred-Year Palace

The One-Hundred-Year Palace is also called the Ten-Thousand-Year Temple. It was built for enshrining the body of the Zen Master Wuxia. It is said that the Zen Master Wuxia was only 26 years old when he came to Mount Jiuhua to practice Buddhism. For many years he lived on wild fruits and spring water. He was sitting cross-legged when he died at the age of 126. His body was kept intact three years after he died. The real body of the Zen Master Wuxia is enshrined in the palace.

附 录 I
Appendix I

中国之最
The Number Ones of China

► 中国面积最大的省区是新疆维吾尔自治区，有 160 万平方千米。

► 中国人口最多的省是河南省，到2005年，有 9 888万人。

► 中国人口最多的城市是上海市，到2005年，有 1 352万人。

► 中国最大的岛屿是台湾岛，面积 3.58 万平方千米。

► 中国最大的群岛是浙江省的舟山群岛，大小岛屿共 670 个，面积 1 200 多平方千米。

► 中国最大的平原是东北平原，面积为 35 万平方千米。

► 中国最大的高原是青藏高原，它也是世界上地势最高的高原，号称"世界屋脊"，面积有 230 万平方千米。

► 中国最高的山峰是珠穆朗玛峰，海拔为 8 844.43 米，也是世界上最高的山峰。

► 中国最大的盆地是塔里木盆地，面积约 53 万平方千米。

► 中国最大的沙漠是塔克拉玛干沙漠，面积 33 万平方千米。

► 中国最长的河流是长江，全长 6 300 千米，也是世界第三长河。

► 中国最大的淡水湖是鄱阳湖，面积约 2 933 平方千米。

► 中国最大的咸水湖和内陆湖是青海省的青海湖，面积 4 340平方千米。

► 中国最深的湖泊是长白山天池，面积9.2平方千米，最深处312.7米。

► 中国海拔最低的湖泊是位于吐鲁番盆地的艾丁湖，湖面低于海平面 155 米，湖底最低处低于海平面 283 米。

► 中国年产量最大的油田是黑龙江省的大庆油田。

► 中国年产量最大的煤田是山西省的大同煤田。

► 中国年吞吐量最大的海港是上海港。

► 中国最热的地方是吐鲁番盆地，7 月平均气温达 33℃，极端最高气温达 49.6℃（1975 年 7 月 13 日）。

► 中国最冷的地方是黑龙江省最北部的漠河县，最低气温达零下 52.3℃（1969 年 2 月 13 日）。

► 中国年降水量最多的地方是台湾省基隆市的火烧寮，年平均降水量为 6 557.8 毫米。

► 中国年降水量最少的地方是新疆塔里木盆地东北部的托克逊

（6.9 毫米），有时常年滴雨不下。

▶ 中国雾日最多的地方是四川省的峨眉山，每年雾日平均达 323.4 天（1953—1980 年）。

▶ The region with the biggest area is Xinjiang Uygur Autonomous Region. It covers 1.60 million km^2.

▶ The province with the largest population is Henan Province, with 98.88 million people by 2005.

▶ The city with the largest population is Shanghai, with 13.52 million people by 2005.

▶ The biggest island is Taiwan Island, with an area of 35 800 km^2.

▶ The biggest archipelago is the Zhoushan Archipelago in Zhejiang Province. It consists of 670 islands with total area of more than 1 200 km^2.

▶ The largest plain is the Northeast Plain, with an area of 350 000 km^2.

▶ The largest plateau is the Qinghai-Tibet Plateau, which is also the highest plateau in the world and reputed to be the roof of the world. It has an area of 2.3 million km^2.

▶ The highest mountain is Mount Qomolangma, with an altitude of 8 844.43 m, which is also the highest mountain in the world.

▶ The largest basin is the Tarim Basin, with an area of about 530 000 km^2.

▶ The biggest desert is the Taklamakan Desert, with an area of 330 000 km^2.

▶ The longest river is the Yangtze River, with a total length of 6 300 km, which is also the third longest river in the world.

▶ The biggest freshwater lake is Poyang Lake, with an area of about 2 933 km^2.

▶ The biggest salt lake and inland lake is Qinghai Lake in Qinghai Province, with an area of 4 340 km^2.

▶ The deepest lake is the Heavenly Pond on Changbai Mountains, with an area of 9.2 km^2 and maximum depth of 312.7 m.

▶ The lowest lake in China is Ayding Lake in the Turpan Depression, which is 155 m below sea level. The deepest place is 283 m below sea level.

▶ The oilfield with the highest annual output is the Daqing Oilfield in Heilongjiang Province.

▶ The coal mine with the highest annual output is the Datong Coal Mine in Shanxi Province.

▶ The port with the largest annual handling capacity is the Shanghai Port.

▶ The hottest place is the Turpan Depression. The average temperature in July reaches 33℃. The highest temperature ever recorded was 49.6℃ on July 13, 1975.

▶ The coldest place is Mohe County in the farthest north of Heilongjiang Province. The lowest temperature is −52.3℃ on February 13, 1969.

▶ The place with the highest annual precipitation is Huoshaoliao in Jilong City of Taiwan, with an average annual precipitation of 6 557.8 mm.

▶ The place with the least annual precipitation(6.9mm) is Toksun northeast of the Tarim Basin in Xinjiang. Sometimes there is no rain throughout the year.

▶ The place with the greatest number of foggy days is Mount Emei in Sichuan Province. There are an average 323.4 foggy days from 1953 to 1980.

附 录 II
Appendix II

中国所拥有的"世界遗产"
The World Heritage in China

名称 Name	所在省、市 Place	性质 Category
长城 The Great Wall	辽宁、河北、北京、山西、内蒙古、宁夏、陕西、甘肃 Liaoning, Hebei, Beijing, Shanxi, Inner Mongolia, Ningxia, Shaanxi, Gansu	世界文化遗产 World Cultural Heritage
明清故宫(北京故宫、沈阳故宫) Imperial Palaces of the Ming and Qing Dynasties in Beijing and Shenyang	北京市、辽宁省 Beijing, Liaoning	世界文化遗产 World Cultural Heritage
天坛 Temple of Heaven: an Imperial Sacrificial Altar in Beijing	北京市 Beijing	世界文化遗产 World Cultural Heritage
周口店北京人遗址 Peking Man Site at Zhoukoudian	北京市 Beijing	世界文化遗产 World Cultural Heritage
颐和园 Summer Palace, an Imperial Garden in Beijing	北京市 Beijing	世界文化遗产 World Cultural Heritage
承德避暑山庄及周围寺庙 Mountain Resort and its Outlying Temples, Chengde	河北省 Hebei Province	世界文化遗产 World Cultural Heritage
秦始皇陵及兵马俑坑 Mausoleum of the First Qin Emperor	陕西省 Shaanxi Province	世界文化遗产 World Cultural Heritage
布达拉宫(大昭寺、罗布林卡) Historic Ensemble of the Potala Palace, Lhasa	西藏自治区 Tibet Autonomous Region	世界文化遗产 World Cultural Heritage
莫高窟 Mogao Caves	甘肃省 Gansu Province	世界文化遗产 World Cultural Heritage
龙门石窟 Longmen Grottoes	河南省 Henan Province	世界文化遗产 World Cultural Heritage
曲阜孔庙、孔林、孔府 Temple and Cemetery of Confucious and the Kong Family Mansion in Qufu	山东省 Shandong Province	世界文化遗产 World Cultural Heritage
泰山 Mount Taishan	山东省 Shandong Province	世界文化与自然遗产 World Cultural and Natural Heritage
平遥古城 Ancient City of Pingyao	山西省 Shanxi Province	世界文化遗产 World Cultural Heritage
苏州古典园林 Classical Gardens of Suzhou	江苏省 Jiangsu Province	世界文化遗产 World Cultural Heritage

名称 Name	所在省、市 Place	性质 Category
明清皇家陵寝 (明显陵、清东陵、清西陵、明孝陵、十三陵、盛京三陵) Imperial Tombs of the Ming and Qing Dynasties	湖北省、河北省、江苏省、北京市、辽宁省 Hubei Province, Hebei Province, Jiangsu Province, Beijing, Liaoning Province	世界文化遗产 World Cultural Heritage
黄山 Mount Huangshan	安徽省 Anhui Province	世界文化与自然遗产 World Cultural and Natural Heritage
皖南古村落 Ancient Villages in South Anhui—Xidi and Hongcun	安徽省 Anhui Province	世界文化遗产 World Cultural Heritage
庐山 Lushan National Park	江西省 Jiangxi Province	世界文化景观 World Cultural Heritage
武夷山 Mount Wuyi	福建省 Fujian Province	世界文化与自然遗产 World Cultural and Natural Heritage
武当山古建筑 Ancient Building Complex in the Wudang Mountains	湖北省 Hubei Province	世界文化遗产 World Cultural Heritage
武陵源 Wulingyuan Scenic and Historic Interest Area	湖南省 Hunan Province	世界自然遗产 World Natural Heritage
峨眉山—乐山大佛 Mount Emei Scenic Area including Leshan Giant Buddha Scenic Area	四川省 Sichuan Province	世界文化与自然遗产 World Cultural and Natural Heritage
黄龙 Huanglong Scenic and Historic Interest Area	四川省 Sichuan Province	世界自然遗产 World Natural Heritage
九寨沟 Jiuzhaigou Valley Scenic and Historic Interest Area	四川省 Sichuan Province	世界自然遗产 World Natural Heritage
大足石刻 Dazu Rock Carvings	重庆市 Chongqing	世界文化遗产 World Cultural Heritage
丽江古城 Old Town of Lijiang	云南省 Yunnan Province	世界文化遗产 World Cultural Heritage
青城山—都江堰 Mount Qingcheng and the Dujiang Irrigation System	四川省 Sichuan Province	世界文化遗产 World Cultural Heritage
云冈石窟 Yungang Grottoes	山西省 Shanxi Province	世界文化遗产 World Cultural Heritage
三江并流 Three Parallel Rivers of Yunnan Protected Areas	云南省 Yunnan Province	世界自然遗产 World Natural Heritage
高句丽王城、王陵及贵族墓葬 Capital Cities and Tombs of the ancient Koguryo Kingdom	吉林省 Jilin Province	世界文化遗产 World Cultural Heritage

名称 Name	所在省、市 Place	性质 Category
澳门历史城区 Historic Center of Macao	澳门特别行政区 Macao SAR	世界文化遗产 World Cultural Heritage
四川大熊猫栖息地 Sichuan Giant Panda Sanctuaries	四川省 Sichuan Province	世界自然遗产 World Natural Heritage
殷墟 Yinxu	河南省 Henan Province	世界文化遗产 World Cultual Heritage

《中国地理常识》

主　　编　焦华富
副主编　洪允智
编写人员　焦华富　方觉曙　李俊峰　赵春雨
责任编辑　金　红
英文编辑　林美琪
美术编辑　阮永贤　刘玉瑜

《中国地理常识》（中英对照）

改编人员　祝　捷　孙飞燕　李水灵　刘晶晶
中文审稿　吴胜明　王树声
英文翻译　王国蕾
英文审稿　许建平　杨纳让　Devon Williams

策　　划　刘　援　祝大鸣
项目负责　祝大鸣　梁　宇
项目编辑　梁　宇
责任编辑　马文敏
版式设计　高等教育出版社美编室
美术编辑　张　楠　赵　阳
封面设计　王凌波
责任绘图　高等教育出版社绘图室
插图选配　马文敏
责任印制　朱学忠
图片来源　高等教育出版社　全景图片公司　ChinaFotoPress

郑 重 声 明

高等教育出版社依法对本书享有专有出版权。任何未经许可的复制、销售行为均违反《中华人民共和国著作权法》，其行为人将承担相应的民事责任和行政责任，构成犯罪的，将被依法追究刑事责任。为了维护市场秩序，保护读者的合法权益，避免读者误用盗版书造成不良后果，我社将配合行政执法部门和司法机关对违法犯罪的单位和个人给予严厉打击。社会各界人士如发现上述侵权行为，希望及时举报，本社将奖励举报有功人员。

反盗版举报电话：（010）58581897/58581896/58581879

反盗版举报传真：（010）82086060

E—mail: dd@hep.com.cn

通信地址：北京市西城区德外大街4号

高等教育出版社打击盗版办公室

邮　　编：100120

购书请拨打电话：（010）58581118

图书在版编目(CIP)数据

中国地理常识/国务院侨务办公室，国家汉语国际推
广领导小组办公室．—北京：高等教育出版社，
2007.2（2010重印）
ISBN 978-7-04-020720-0

Ⅰ．中… Ⅱ．①国…②国… Ⅲ．①汉语－对外汉
语教学－语言读物②地理－基本知识－中国－汉、英
Ⅳ．① H195.5 ② K92

中国版本图书馆 CIP 数据核字(2006)第 128486 号

出版发行	高等教育出版社		购书热线	010 - 58581118
社　　址	北京市西城区德外大街4号		免费咨询	800 - 810 - 0598
邮政编码	100120		网　　址	http://www.hep.edu.cn
总　　机	010-58581000			http://www.hep.com.cn
			网上订购	http://www.landraco.com
经　　销	蓝色畅想图书发行有限公司			http://www.landraco.com.cn
印　　刷	北京信彩瑞禾印刷厂		畅想教育	http://www.widedu.com
开　　本	787 × 1092　1/16		版　　次	2007 年 2 月第 1 版
印　　张	17		印　　次	2010 年 1 月第 12 次印刷
字　　数	380 000			

本书如有印装等质量问题，请到所购图书销售部门调换。　　ISBN 978-7-04-020720-0
06200